GET MORE OUT OF YOUR
MARCO POLO

KU-675-097

IT'S AS SIMPLE AS THIS

1 go.marco-polo.com/oxf

2 download and discover

GO!

WORKS OFFLINE!

SYMBOLS

INSIDER TIP Insider Tip

★ Highlight

●●●● Best of ...

☆ Scenic view

☺ Responsible travel: fair
   trade principles and the
   environment respected

(*) Telephone numbers
   that are not toll-free

PRICE CATEGORIES HOTELS

Expensive	over £200
Moderate	£120–200
Budget	to £120

The prices are for two people
sharing per night, including
breakfast

PRICE CATEGORIES RESTAURANTS

Expensive	over £20
Moderate	£10–20
Budget	under £10

The prices are for a standard
main course without drinks

DID YOU KNOW?
Fit in the city → p. 49
Favourite eateries → p. 54
Specialities → p. 56
Spotlight on sports → p. 67
Time to chill → p. 79
More than a good night's
sleep → p. 84
Mayday, Mayday → p. 100
Public holidays → p. 105
Budgeting → p. 109
For bookworms and film
buffs → p. 110

Currency converter → p. 111
Weather → p. 112

MAPS IN THE GUIDEBOOK
(116 A1) Page numbers and
coordinates refer to the city
atlas
Coordinates are also given for
places that are not marked in
the city atlas

(0) Site/address located off
the map

Map of Oxford and surround-
ings p. 124/125

(🔯 A–B 2–3) refers to the
removable pull-out map

INSIDE FRONT COVER:
The best Highlights

INSIDE BACK COVER:
Public transport

The best MARCO POLO Insider Tips

Our Top 15 Insider Tips

INSIDER TIP Vacancies

Stay at a college: When the students have gone home, you can contact *University Rooms* for an authentic, rather reasonable – and unique! – place to stay → p. 84

INSIDER TIP Tennis with a difference

Forget about Wimbledon... Real Tennis is more real, older and – above all – cooler! One of the few remaining courts is at Merton College → p. 25

INSIDER TIP Carver Alice

Who the **** is Alice? Alice Liddell was the real-life model for Lewis Carroll's "Alice in Wonderland" – and in her spare time she also produced first-class wood carvings. At *St Frideswide's Church* you can admire a door panel she made → p. 46

INSIDER TIP Art at Pizza Express

Not fast food: take the time to enjoy your meal at the Italian restaurant in the *Golden Cross Passage* and admire the original murals on the walls, which date back to Tudor times → p. 55

INSIDER TIP Secret Garden

Wild flowers thrive on the river bank, swans glide past, and there's a small bench under the cherry tree: recharge your batteries in the enchanted *garden of Lady Margaret Hall* → p. 94

INSIDER TIP Dinner on the roof terrace

From coffee to a gourmet meal: in the rooftop restaurant *Benugo* at the *Ashmolean Museum*, the dining is high up, exclusive, and accompanied by jazz – with five floors of art and culture beneath you (photo right) → p. 42

INSIDER TIP Cricket for free

You can watch top-calibre players in the *University Parks* (photo top) free of charge. What were the rules again? → p. 41

BEST OF ...

FOR FREE

● *Chasing after the golden snitch*
Quidditch is for Muggles as well as for the students at Hogwarts.
There are even world championships in this unusual type of sport.
Would you like to watch? *No problem* – there are two practices a
week at the University Parks → p. 24

● *College choir in the chapel*
You must see this: the heavenly sound of *Evensong* will resound in
your ears for a long time – a festive, solemn (and free!) experience
→ p. 70

● *Pure multi-culture*
Trendy? Always. Spend a lot of money? Never! The graffiti-flanked
façades of *Cowley Road* (photo) delight with their popular hipster
shops and international restaurants. All sorts of fabulous things at
low prices, culinary treats from all over the world to enjoy and fill
up on – and that won't break the bank → p. 45

● *Prints that make an impression*
Michelangelo, Raphael and all the others: normally you have
to spend quite a lot of money to see the Old Masters – but not
at the Ashmolean Museum, which also has art for the money-
conscious → p. 42

● *College secrets*
Medieval cottages, an enchanted garden, fabulous/
crazy chapel: step through the gate of *Worcester
College*, and you step into a different world – and
it won't cost you a penny → p. 45

● *Picture postcard*
Mind your step – the view will bowl you over!
From *Christ Church Meadow*, take a look
back at the zigzags of the college towers to
the south of the old town. You can take this
mental image home with you as a souvenir
→ p. 31

●●●● Dots in guidebook refer to 'Best of' tips

● *Fun in a punt*

When you go punting (photo), you push your boat forward with a long pole! It's romantic, entertaining, wobbly, and sometimes wet – but always plenty of fun – and what could be more typical! → p. 49

● *Grotesque grimaces*

They've got their eye on you: Oxford's mischievous/demonic *gargoyles* look down on you from up high. And whether they're spouting water or not, it's always worth looking up to see them → p. 21

● *Double-decker double tour*

City tour deluxe: opt for the *Hop-on-hop-off double-decker bus* to save yourself from getting blisters on your feet – with the added benefit of enjoying the fresh breeze on the open deck. All the sights, two routes, one price → p. 113

● *All tied up*

At the cosy *The Bear* you'll find thousands of ties on the walls – happily exchanged by enthusiastic beer-lovers for a *pint*. Not a bad deal! → p. 77

● *Maze of antiques*

Are you looking for a floppy hat, an Art Deco necklace or an orchestral score from the 17th century? If you can't find what you're looking for at *Antiques on High*, you won't find it anywhere. Browse the tiny nooks and crannies in peace: over 25 dealers have everything from crazy stuff to valuable collector's items → p. 61

● *From a unicorn to a no-horn*

Mythical creatures, a Harry Potter backdrop, a squeaky hill – you'll be hard pressed to find anywhere more offbeat than medieval, venerable *New College* even in Oxford → p. 37

● *Bumps-a-daisy*

Bump! The spectator sport in Oxford that beats all the others. Not a body part, nothing slippery, and not a Seventies retro dance, but: rowing regatta! *Torpids* and *Summer Eights* – iconic "bumps" boating races with the college teams on the Isis → p. 67

BEST OF ...

● *Shopping for non-shoppers*
Pioneering shopping mall *The Covered Market* (photo) has been around for 250 years. It has all sorts of interesting items for shopaholics – and plenty of history for the non-shoppers – under one roof → p. 64

● *Art house in an Art Deco cinema*
Coffee and cake and cult films are all on offer here at the *Ultimate Picture Palace*. The historical cinema with a moving history is a lovely place to visit → p. 75

● *Books on chains*
Harry Potter backdrop, storage for ancient tomes, state-of-the-art research centre: you'll see and learn so much on a *guided tour* of the *Bodleian Library* → p. 36

● *Shrunken heads etc.*
Still need a dried toad for your magic potion? The lovely staff at the *Pitt Rivers Museum* will be pleased to show you entire drawers full of interesting objects, as well as other curiosities from the chamber of horrors → p. 41

● *Refreshments in style*
Coffee to go – no, thank you! Guests at the lavishly styled *The Grand Café* take their time. Make your choice from the selection of cakes on the baroque marble counter, order a pot of tea to go with it – or perhaps even a glass of Champagne. The perfect treat for a rainy day – or indeed any kind of day! → p. 51

● *Urge to play*
Bored? Then go for board – game, that is: at the *Thirsty Meeples* games café, you can choose from thousands of them. Just to try them out, to play there or even take them with you if you like → p. 54

RAIN

RELAX AND CHILL OUT
Take it easy and spoil yourself

● *There is a green field...*
It's not a long walk *to Port Meadow* – the large, ancient meadow of open common land beside the River Thames is a lovely spot to relax right near the city. Cattle, horses, wild flowers alongside the river – and the city stress is forgotten → p. 46

● *Boat trip*
Glide slowly along the Thames – with photo ops just waiting for you around every bend. There is no more relaxed way to experience Oxford than on a *river cruise* → p. 113

● *Cocktails with a view*
You sit right amongst the "dreaming spires" on the roof terrace of the *Varsity Club* (photo): chillax with a cool drink and fabulous views → p. 74

● *A spot under a linden tree*
Relax, chat to a loved one, look around you, enjoy nature: All this awaits at the idyllic *Havel's Place* in the University Parks. The work of art beside the pond belongs to a group of similar works all over the world, and is intended to be used! → p. 41

● *Teatime at the Grand Hotel*
The epitome of style and charm: luxurious *afternoon tea* in the Drawing Room of the *Randolph Hotel*. Enjoy scones, sandwiches and bubbly – accompanied by a piano on Saturdays. Heavenly!
→ p. 83

● *Sink down into your chair*
The reading room above the *Turl Street Kitchen* has comfortable leather sofas that are perfect for relaxing. Lose yourself in a good book beside the open fire and plan your next moves in your exploration of Oxford... perhaps this one?!
→ p. 57

11

DISCOVER OXFORD!

Enchanting Oxford – the city of secrets: a portal to the magical world of Harry Potter with chained books, wood-panelled dining halls and winding staircases to wind-swept turret rooms. *Students in flapping gowns* cycle over the bumpy lanes, thick-walled colleges sit cheek by jowl, grotesque gargoyles on the *Gothic jagged turrets* look down on the medieval city from above: this postcard image is synonymous with Oxford all over the world. Romantic Oxford: "Sweet city of dreaming spires", as the poet Matthew Arnold put it. But if you're picturing a sleepy nest, you are absolutely on the wrong track. Oxford is ancient and post-modern, *venerable and goofy*, elegant and vulgar, lovely and ugly, and everything in between. The spires may indeed be dreaming, but no one else is! The things that have gone – and go – on here often defy description!

But let's start at the beginning: the "ford of the oxen" was a river crossing for oxen around 900 AD. Ever heard of St Frideswide, princess, nun and the patron saint of Oxford? In the early Middle ages, one Algar, King of Leicester, harassed the unap-proachable beauty relentlessly, until God had finally had enough and punished the irritating would-be suitor by striking him blind. Unfortunately, though, God didn't check things with Frideswide first, but simply set about making Algar blind – an act that she, in turn, thought was perhaps a bit much. So she did what anyone would have done in this situation: *she had water spring forth from a holy spring,* which restored Algar's sight. Then she quickly founded a convent, and the rest is history!

In order to understand Oxford, though, you need to understand the complicated relationship between the city and the university – "town and gown". The city (town) and university (the academic gown) have been at *loggerheads since the year dot* – and often it was a matter of life and death. In 1209, fearful "gownies" fled north after yet another battle with the "townies", and founded a brand-new university there. And what was the name of the unknown little town they headed for? Cambridge!

Town and gown in constant strife

Things got really bad again in Oxford on St Scholastica's Day in 1355: a fight at the Swyndlestock Tavern on Carfax developed into full-on violence – the townies killed no fewer than 63 students – and almost 500 years later, every single citizen still had to pay the university 63 pennies as a collective penalty. The king sided with the university: *gown now had almost total power over town,* and also a say in municipal matters, such as determining prices and weights, or arranging for the streets to be cleaned. The situation remains tense between the two to this day.

Oxford is the oldest university in any English-speaking country. Its roots are actually the result of a fight between France and England. In 1167, to annoy King Henry II, the University of Paris expelled all English people. They returned home, and settled in Oxford. As luck would have it, there were already a few religious institutions here, and over time these became the first colleges. The often biblical names, and the academic gowns that resemble a monk's habit, still bear witness to this today. *Religion was often essential in Oxford:* during the Reformation, people as well as books were burnt, depending on the ideology – gruesome. The most famous victims were the Bishops Cranmer, Latymer and Ridley. A cobbled cross in the middle of Broad Street is a memorial to the site where, under the

Cornmarket Street – popular shopping street with a view of the Tom Tower of Christ Church

Catholic queen "Bloody Mary", the three Protestant "heretics" came to such a terrible end on a pyre.

The university still dominates the city, although it is essentially a concept and not a specific building: Oxford University consists of 38 colleges scattered all over the city. Each college has its own identity, *including whimsical customs and habits*. Oxford University is state-owned; like all the other universities in England, the annual fees for students from the UK and Europe are £9,250 for a Bachelor's course. Students from other countries pay significantly more. There are plenty of applicants, simply because no matter which ratings list you choose, Oxford will invariably be right at the top of it. Without top marks, you cannot expect to be offered a place. And once you have your place, the battle is by no means over: the standards are extremely high. Over half of Britain's Prime Ministers are ex-Oxonians, including Theresa May, David Cameron, Tony Blair and Margaret Thatcher.

Oxford is a young, dynamic city

However, the world-famous elite university is not the only university in the city: there is also the Oxford Brookes University, with four separate campuses. The large number of students makes Oxford (pop. 158,000) a young, dynamic and multifaceted city. It has a total of over 40,000 students – fewer during the summer holidays between July and September, but then it has thousands of young language students who want to improve their English. Students often live in the college or in halls of residence to begin with, and later on move out into shared accommodation in the city. Very popular with students: trendy Jericho and the dynamic, alternative Cowley Road.

> **Alongside the traditional privileges of the wealthy elite there are social problem areas**

The main employers in Oxford are the NHS (National Health Service), the educational facilities, research and technology, publishing and – of course – tourism. Every year, around seven million visitors come to the university city to see the highly traditional colleges and experience the unique atmosphere. The wealthy colleges are impressive in their medieval magnificence, and even within the UK *Oxford is regarded as posh*. However, the city also has to battle with a number of challenges. Performance at its schools is below the national average, and a number of suburbs in the south and east are amongst the weakest socially in all of England. One in four of its children is growing up in poverty, and one-fifth of its adults has no, or only very poor, qualifications. Social problem areas coexist alongside the traditional privileges of the wealthy elite. Generally, the better-off live in the northern part of the city, in Jericho and Summertown, while the poorer people live in the south and east, e.g. Cowley. One constant topic of conversation is the extremely high cost of living. Oxford is at risk of flooding, the centre of the city is listed, and it is surrounded by a greenbelt – there is little space for new residential areas, and the current ones are amongst the most expensive in Great Britain.

> **Medieval colleges and 'in' quarters**

To experience the true spirit of Oxford, you need to let the fundamentally different areas work their magic on you. In the centre of the city, the medieval colleges with their chapels and jagged spires cluster around historic High Street. The heart of the small, historic old town is easy to explore on foot. A walk at twilight is particularly atmospheric, *when the retro street lamps shine their dim light on the thick, ancient walls* and the Gothic embellishments strike a bizarre contrast to the intensely coloured sky. With its spires and medieval atmosphere, Oxford has inspired poets of all ages, and is also a popular film location – and not just for the Harry Potter films! Stroll around Radcliffe Square in the heart of the old town, with the iconic circular structure of the Radcliffe Camera and views of the centuries-old university buildings – it will take your breath away. To the north is the hip suburb of Jericho with its artisan foodie shops and lamp-lit Little Clarendon Street, while to the east is colourful, *dynamic Cowley Road* with its authentic multi-cultural atmosphere, trendy bars and restaurants, and cool street art. The romantic parks and meadows

Where to put all the books? Radcliffe Camera became the reading room of the Bodleian Library in 1890

scattered around and the waterways, with punts gliding by, complete the image of Oxford as a picturesque town in a typically English setting.

In contrast to this stand the scientific research institutes and technology centres. They are ultra-modern and amongst the best in the world, but the sights, cultural institutions and service sector are also bang up-to-date and frequently active on social media such as Facebook, Twitter and Instagram. The buildings are also being prettified. It started with the castle area, where the aim was to achieve a contemporary, sustainable and attractive restoration; the railway station came next. *The colleges are being given post-modern extensions and conversions,* while the futuristic Blavatnik School of Government and the new Westgate Mall demonstrate that old and new can be a creative combination.

And when you've had enough of the venerable history and tour of the city? Then ground yourself over a real ale in a cosy pub or a summery Pimm's on a punt, rock some festivals, and dance under the rainbow at the Cowley Road Carnival. Oxford simply has it all – see for yourself how this little city manages to create a unique and unforgettable "whole" from so many different aspects! *See you later!*

WHAT'S HOT

1 Grow your own

Allotment gardening Are allotments a conventional hell for garden gnomes? No way! If Oxfordians decide they want a green patch in the mini garden colony, they need to be patient and go on the waiting list. Then, when they have their fertile patch of soil, they relish the sustainable trend for growing their own organic carrots, potatoes, pumpkins and all the other delights that flourish in Oxford's climate zone. And the people who don't grow their own can buy from the people that do: the *Veg Van* of *Cultivate Oxford* (www.cultivateoxford. org) brings the produce into the city. At *Incredible Edible Oxford* (short.travel/oxf13), people can learn things like how to garden for their own requirements and how to build a beehive.

2

Mastermind

Good luck! Who doesn't love a quiz? And when you find yourself amidst the buildings that spawned the winning team for this year's University Challenge, perhaps you fancy your chances? But keep it simple – quiz nights at the pub are endlessly popular and usually full to bursting. Try Wednesday at the *Prince of Wales* (8.30pm | £2 | 73 Church Way, Iffley Village | www.princeatiffley.co.uk) or Thursdays at the *Fir Tree* (8.30pm | 163 Iffley Road | www.facebook.com/firtreeoxford).

3 1, 2, 3 testing

Is this thing on? On *Open Mic Nights* anyone can take to the microphone! At the trendy *Catweazle Club* (Thu 8pm–11pm, registration until 7.30pm | £6 | East Oxford Community City | 44b Princes Street | tel. 01865 792168 | www.catweazleclub. com), budding performers cluster around the stage on Thursdays. Unplugged and unamplified, they can do exactly as they please. The only risk: being booed off. Music, song, poetry, comedy – anything goes! Some people make the cut, such as singer-songwriter Rhys Lewis, but most of the hopefuls are never heard of again – and often that's no bad thing. The *Harcourt Arms* (Sun 7.30pm–10.30pm | Cranham, Jericho | www. harcourtarmsjericho.co.uk) specialises in music, the *James Street Tavern* (Thu 8pm–10pm | 47–48 James Street) in comedy, and the *Half Moon* (Sun 9pm–midnight | 18 St Clements Street | short.travel/oxf14) in Irish Folk.

Om in the City

New centre From awareness to Zen – concepts that nourish the soul are in. At *Inner Space (daily 10am–6pm, appointment not necessary | guided meditation 12.30pm–1pm and 5.30pm–6pm | no charge | 21 Broad Street | www.innerspace.org/oxford),* visitors leave the stress of the city outside and seek inner focus in this peaceful haven. On Saturday mornings, people gather between 11.30am and 12.30pm for meditative Sahaja Yoga at the *Friends Meeting House* (43 Saint Giles | no charge | short.travel/oxf15). Namaste!

Group dosh

Crowdfunding What to do when there's no money? Clear: if everyone pitches in, then there will automatically be more cash in the coffers. Crowdfunded projects in Oxford include the £26,000 Master's Degree for Emily-Rose Eastop, who thought it's worth a try – and it was! – and a sustainable residential development by Kevin McCloud, the TV property expert. Go to *short.travel/oxf16* to see what projects are listed in this innovative way to raise money.

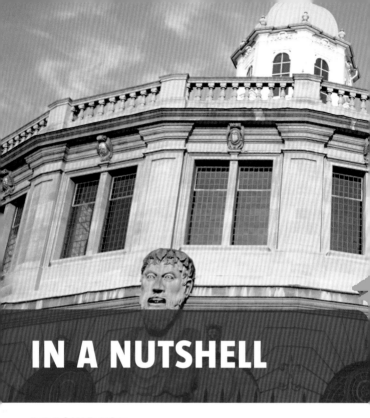

IN A NUTSHELL

WOULD YOU BELIEVE IT

Oxford is famous for all sorts of strange customs and habits – and every college has its own quirks. What do you mean – Rosa Luxemburg was at Balliol? Oh yes, but it's not what you think: Rosa was a tortoise. Several colleges keep these cute little land-dwelling reptiles, and hold races with them. A Communist wind blows at Balliol with regard to tortoises: the little creatures are named after party members, and are cared for by a *comrade tortoise*.

Think the Jesus College flag looks a little strange? Then it'll be St David's Day, and there will be a leek (the national symbol of Wales) on the mast in homage to the college's Welsh roots.

All Souls, the exclusive research institute and stronghold of the international uber-intelligentsia, is the site of a surreal duck hunt: *Hunting the Mallard*. It is said that in 1437, during the building works, said *mallard* flew out of a drain. The event has been celebrated ever since, led by a ceremonial *Lord of the Mallard*, a wacky ritual for this bird with a lantern-led procession and specially composed duck song. You'd like to experience it? Better put it in your calendar now, then: 14 January, 2101. *Hunting the Mallard* only takes place every hundred years!

GARGLING GNOME

Feel like you're being followed?! Unlikely! Look up – and you'll probably

Eccentric customs, strange sport, cheeky gargoyles, stronghold of education since the Middle Ages

encounter various demonically grinning, grotesque faces: ★ ● gargoyles! The name is based on the word *gargle*, and strictly speaking gargoyles spout water, while their cousins (the grotesques) only give the evil eye. This is far from being a short-lived design trend: back in the 12th century it was customary to adorn churches with shifty creatures from the world of horror fantasy, the idea being: you stay outside! So are they all medieval fantasy creatures? No, not at all – along with the winged gob-

lins, nose-picking dwarfs and obscene gnomes, there are also quite a few contemporary faces with glasses or squash racquets. The Bodleian Library recently held a competition for the next generation – and the results can now be seen at lofty heights in the Schools Quad. The most bizarre gargoyles can be seen on University Church, in New College Lane, Queens Lane and in Turl Street. Happy hunting! But before you rush to click on "Like" for the Oxford Gargoyles on Facebook, have a closer look: you won't

Can still be admired in its natural environment here: original retro phone box

be "liking" the mischievous decorative figures, but the à capella group of the same name.

DESIGN ICONS ON THE STREET

Did you know that in Oxford, the red telephone boxes are listed? These brightly-coloured iconic boxes designed by Gilbert Scott are facing extinction all over the UK, but 13 of them have the great good fortune to see out their (well-earned) retirement in the midst of the medieval colleges. But that's not to say that they're not working: most of them can still be used as usual! And where are they? Well, scattered all over the city centre, for instance on High Street, Broad Street, Catte Street or right in front of the Carfax Tower, the most central point in Oxford. You can't miss them. But that's not to say that any two *phone boxes* are the same: communications design nerds will instantly be able to distinguish between a 1924 K2, and a 1935 K6. Do you have to hold an ear-piece to your ear, and ask the young lady to connect you? Nonsense – the technology is absolutely up-to-date. However, conservationists should still watch out: the former state telephone company British Telecom keeps trying to replace these iconic little boxes with modern ones – which is hardly surprising, because true connoisseurs will spend large quantities of money on these obsolete treasures! And be honest, how cool do they look as a garden feature or a shower cabin? But here in Oxford, the originals are fairly safe: so far, as soon as anyone tries to do anything to one of these popular symbols of Britain, a throng of intrepid citizens organises a successful protest campaign. Another lucky escape!

HIGH SCHOOL OF SUCCESS

Would you like to study in Oxford?

There's nothing stopping you! Every summer, the *Oxford University Summer School for Adults (www.conted.ox.ac.uk/about/oussa)* offers short courses. What can the fossils of the Cretaceous Period tell us? What do the top Tudor hits for the viola sound like? You can debate questions such as these and others with Oxford professionals and inquisitive kindred spirits. It will cost you from £1,120 a week, including meals and accommodation at Rewley House, Wellington Square.

Doesn't suit your schedule? Then register for a *MOOC*! The *Massive Open Online Course (free, optional verified certificate for a fee | www.edx.org)*, it is the ultimate in the learning revolution – anyone can join in online and free of charge. Oxford Uni jumped on the MOOC bandwagon in 2017 – how about you?

THRONE OF THE YEAR

And the winner is... Oxford! The city is quite rightly proud of its award; after all, it invested £700,000 and outdid many other high-calibre competitors. In 2016, the British Toilet Association awarded the city ten Platinum and eight Gold awards, making it the absolute outright winner in the category of "loos". Did you know: not only are there some wonderful "smallest rooms" in the Town Hall, the three parks and four cemeteries, at the Redbridge Park-and-Ride and 14 others in the heart of the city, but also plenty in various cafés, restaurants and shops. *You're welcome to use our facilities!* Wherever you see this sentence on blue-and-white stickers, you can relieve yourself free of charge, and with absolutely no obligation to make a purchase. Good ones are at *Marks & Spencer (Queen Street)* and *Pizza Hut (George Street)* – barrier-free and with baby changing facilities.

SHELLEY'S BEST PIECE

At *University College*, it's worth having a look at the first *quad* around the next corner on the right. This is where you will find the sculpture, as naked as on the day he was born, of the drowned poet Percy Bysshe Shelley, dramatically draped over his mausoleum. The latter is only a prop, though: Edward Onslow Ford's sculpture of the ex-Romantic turned out to be both too large and too naked for Shelley's actual burial site on the Protestant cemetery in Rome. Significantly, what the memorial inscription here at the uni omits to say is that the college threw Shelley out after only two terms, as he had made himself unpopular with his "rebellious" behaviour and atheist pamphlets. Student pranksters like to pay attention to one particular part of the marble figure's anatomy: from time to time, you'll be able to see Shelley's "best piece" in all its glory and painted blue.

WOMAN POWER

To tremendous protest of their male counterparts, in 1878 the first female students moved into the macho stronghold that was Oxford University – fraternity was the order of the day among the exclusively male students who had studied there for 700 years. To ensure that everything remained patriarchally unchanged, various rather dubious arguments were bandied about, such as "studying leaves you infertile" (that only applied to women, of course). Yet surely one would expect these people, more than any others, to know that education is far from being an ideal form of contraception: in the 17th century, a girl disguised as a man crept into St Edmund Hall and was only unmasked when her room neighbour got her pregnant. Silly mistake! But slowly, slowly,

Oxford is always a popular Harry Potter location, and not just at Halloween

equality crept into the university, and today all the colleges are co-educational. Not only that, but since 2016 there has been a woman at the helm: Professor Louise Richardson.

SPORT OF MUGGLES

With a *broom* between their legs and irritated by constant Bludger attacks, six Chasers, four Beaters, two Keepers and two Seekers fight for the Quaffle. Watch out – here comes the Snitch Runner! If you think Harry Potter is about to come whizzing down from above on a Nimbus 2000 to catch the Golden Snitch and throw it through one of the opponents' three hoops, then you're not that far off the mark: this is nothing other than

● *Quidditch*. Of course, the brooms don't really fly, but nonetheless the game is taken completely seriously. From 2pm on Wednesdays and Saturdays (term-time only), the Radcliffe Chimeras and Oxford Quidlings from the *Oxford University Quidditch Club (www.ouqc.uk)* practise in the University Parks. At the last world championship in Frankfurt, the UK came third after the USA and the current champion, Australia. Good luck with your training!

SPORT OF KINGS

It might not be magic, but *Real Tennis* is no less quirky. Everything is off-centre and warped: the racquets, the hall and the net. The fun starts with the serve: the *service styles* have crazy names like *railroad, bobble, poop, piqué, boomerang* and *giraffe*. "Real" comes from the word "royal": Henry VIII was a fan – but perhaps his six wives would have done better to let him win? There are still 24 courts in the UK, and one of them – naturally – is in Oxford! Opposite Merton College on Merton Street you'll find INSIDER TIP a small shop run by the Oxford University Tennis Club. You are most welcome to call in and ask if anyone is playing – if you're in luck, you'll be taken through a club house that strongly resembles a living room, and will be able to watch really close up – perhaps even too close? *New balls please!*

MARGINAL: M&S IS SHOCK-RESISTANT

The Oxford M&S on Queen's Street looks pretty much like all the others, with one exception that is hidden away in the far-left corner near the Food Hall. There you will see a glass display cabinet with a chunky piece of light yellow stone with a hammered inscription. Whaaaa...? Yup; it is a testimony to one of Oxford's many unusual customs: *beating the bounds*, or "setting the boundaries". And this piece of stone is a boundary stone that used to delineate the old parish boundaries. Every year on *Ascension Day* in May, a delegation from the parish moves from boundary stone to boundary stone, regardless of whether shops, homes or anything else have been built over them in the meantime. This is where the beating comes into play: the troop bangs on the boundary markers with sticks and calling, *"mark, mark, mark"*. No, it's nothing to do with the name of the store, but rather something that has been left over from the Mid-

dle Ages, the days before Google Maps, when people had to check the boundaries differently. The exact spot at M&S is marked by a brass cross in the ground – look out for it, next time you pop in to check the underwear. *Doesn't everyone?*

DO YOU SPEAK OXFORD?

Do you speak Oxford English? Then you have a very posh accent. An "Oxford comma" is useful when listening, but basically optional, and grammatically somewhat debatable (psst! that was one just now!). "Oxford Blue" is both the dark-blue trademark colour of the university as well as a person who represents it in a competition, such as the Oxford *Cambridge Boat Race* (now renamed the *Cancer Research UK Boat Race*). It's not just the clocks that tick differently in Oxford, but the directions are also different: wherever you come from, you always say you're going *up* to Oxford if you're going there, and *down* if you're leaving it. Someone who has been *sent down* is considered by the "dons", the university academics, to have been thrown out. And the pronunciation? If you say "Ox-ford" rather than "Ox-fudd", you will immediately give yourself away as a non-native. The Thames is called the Isis here, and the River Cherwell is pronounced "Charwell". It gets trickier with Magdalen: never say "Mag-da-len"; it's always "Mawd-lin" – unless you're in C... in the other university city! Sub-fusc (from the Latin for "dark colour") is the black gown that the students have to wear on formal occasions (often, then). Final tip: whatever you do, don't add a completely superfluous "college" to the name Christ Church. *"Good luck with your Oxford English!"*

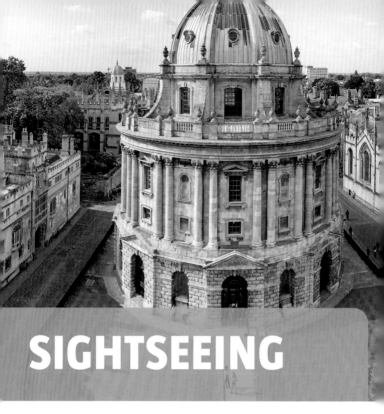

SIGHTSEEING

It's a well-known fact that Oxford is an elite university city. However, most visitors are less interested in modern

CITY **WHERE TO START?**
Dominated by the impressive Radcliffe Camera and St Mary's Gothic spire, Radcliffe Square **(122 B3)** *(∅ F6)* is the perfect starting point. You're right at the heart of the old town here, surrounded by medieval colleges and other thick-walled university buildings. To the north lies Broad Street, which is flanked by colleges, and to the south is the historic High Street.

laboratories and high-tech equipment, and more so in its historic buildings with a Harry Potter ambience – all snuggled together on about half a square mile around the 1,000-year-old High Street. The basic elements of a college are: the square courtyard, the *quadrangles*, *quads* for short; the *dining hall*, and the *chapel*. Students live and learn in the colleges, although visitors don't usually get to see their rooms, which are arranged around staircases. Porters sit at the entrance and decide who is allowed to go in – the doors are closed when darkness falls. It is also possible that even during the official opening hours, you might find a sign saying, *"The college is closed to visitors"* at the entrance *(for*

Dreaming spires, venerable colleges, museums: and amongst them all, natural oases and idyllic waterways

information and the opening hours of all the colleges go to short.travel/oxf1). But Oxford is much more than a bundle of colleges in the old town. There are affluent residential areas to the north and north-west, and in particular the trendy suburb of Jericho, while to the south-east the areas along and around multi-cultural Cowley Road are more socially mixed. Lots of parks and meadows, and picturesque waterways contribute to Oxford's idyllic, relaxed appeal.

OLD TOWN: UP AND DOWN HIGH STREET

The medieval centre is home to the jewels of Oxford's architectural treasures, including the magnificent College Christ Church and Gothic St Mary's.

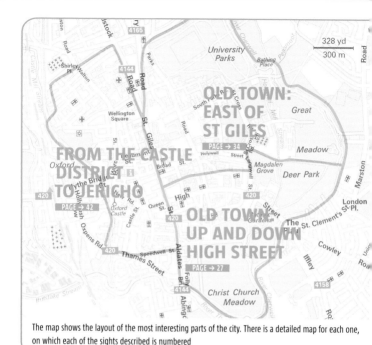

The map shows the layout of the most interesting parts of the city. There is a detailed map for each one, on which each of the sights described is numbered

The much-lauded and now traffic-free High Street, usually called *The High* for short, is the main artery of the historic centre.

■ BOTANIC GARDEN
(122 C3–4) (*M* G6–7)

England's oldest botanic garden was developed as a scientific university garden on what had been the Jewish cemetery in the Middle Ages. Enchanted paths and gnarled trees from the 17th century combined with a modern kitchen garden and greenhouses full of tropical plants – there's something very special about this spot beside the Cherwell. You're not allowed to touch or pick the plants – and especially not the cannabis in the medicinal section!

The garden has often played a literary role. Near the water garden at the north end is the INSIDER TIP famous bench where Lara and Will from Philip Pullman's Northern Lights trilogy meet in two different dimensions. Tip: The ticket office is closed on weekdays in December and January, so entry is free. For families there is the *family trail* (information in the office), following a separate route. The Big Botanic backpacks (no charge for borrowing) are full of materials that you can use to actively explore the garden. *Jun–Aug daily 9am–6pm, Mar/Apr, Sep/Oct Mon noon–5pm, Tue–Sun 9am–5pm, May Mon noon–6pm, Tue–Sun 9am–6pm, Nov–Feb Mon noon–4pm, Tue–Sun 9am–4pm | Guided tours in summer Thu, Sat 11.30am,*

2pm (1 hour, £2.50 plus admission) | £5 | Rose Lane | tel. 01865 286690 | www.botanic-garden.ox.ac.uk

▣ BRASENOSE COLLEGE
(122 B3) (*ΩΩ F6*)

Trust us, and come with us! Go from the Porter's Lodge directly to the Old Quad, then straight to the far-right corner. Now – and only now; definitely no sooner – turn around, and look back to the entrance. Well? Did we promise too much? The `INSIDER TIP` view from here of the Radcliffe Camera and the tower of St Mary's is simply breathtaking.

Odd name, though, isn't it – Brasenose? But it does literally come from *brass* and *nose*: brass nose! It refers to a door knocker, an unidentified animal with a ring through its nose – you can see it in the Dining Hall behind the High Table. Apparently, this nasal door knocker was purloined in 1333 by "rebellious students and dons", and carried off to Stamford in Lincolnshire. 550 years later (!) it turned up there on the door of an old schoolhouse. "It's ours," said Brasenose College, and without further ado bought the entire school. They've got their noses out in front, those Brasenosers! *Mon–Fri 10–11.30am, 2–4.30pm, Sat/Sun 9.30–10.30am (11.30am in the holidays), 2pm–4.30pm (5pm in summer | £2 | Radcliffe Square | www.bnc.ox.ac.uk*

▣ CHRIST CHURCH ★
(122 B3–4) (*ΩΩ F6–7*)

The biggest, richest, most impressive and most famous of the Oxford colleges, nickname: *The House*. The porters wear bowler hats, and the clocks are all slow: every evening at five past nine, *Great Tom* chimes 101 times in memory of the number of the first students in 1525 – and Oxford Time is five minutes behind Greenwich Mean Time! Harry Potter fans will recognise Christ Church by the unbeatable dining room (even though

MARCO POLO HIGHLIGHTS

it, along with an additional table, was rebuilt in the film studio) and by the fabulous staircase. Charming detail on the latter: the brass dragons on the gaslights. On the staircase, don't miss the door with the inscription *"No Peel"*: this was a protest in 1829 against Robert Peel, the then Home Secretary.

An extremely creative and versatile maths professor at Christ Church, author, photographer and preacher called Charles Dodgson invented (amongst other things!) the nyctograph (a device for writing in the dark), travel chess sets, a precursor to Scrabble, and: the stories of Alice in Wonderland. Under the pseudonym Lewis Carroll, Charles immortalised many Oxford curiosities in his surreal stories, from Christ Church e.g. **INSIDER TIP** the long necks of the fire-dogs in the Great Hall.

Christ Church Cathedral is both the city's main church and college chapel. Its main attractions are the reconstructed St Frideswide shrine, the windows by the pre-Raphaelites William Morris and Edmund Burne-Jones, and windows with glass embellishments from the Middle Ages. *College Mon–Sat 10am–5pm, Sun 2pm–5pm | Cathedral Mon–Sat 10am–4.15pm, Sun 2pm–4.15pm | £7–9 depending on the month | St Aldate's (entrance from Christ Church Meadow in Meadow Gate) | www.chch.ox.ac.uk*

Behind the façade of Christ Church College is a small private art gallery: the *Christ Church Picture Gallery*. In changing cycles, you can admire works by van Dyck, Frans Hals, Rubens and other masters. *Opening hours similar to the College, but closed Tue from Oct-Jun | £4 | Free guided tours Mon 2.30pm | Entrance in Canterbury Quad during a college tour, or separate entrance through Canterbury Gate. Oriel Square (corner Oriel Street/Merton Street) | www.chch.ox.ac.uk/gallery*

Christ Church – THE showcase college of Oxford

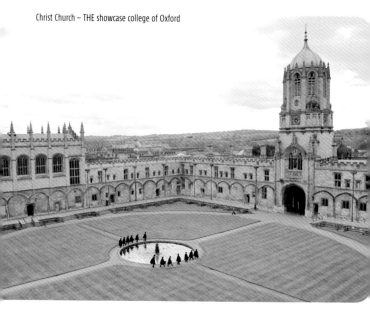

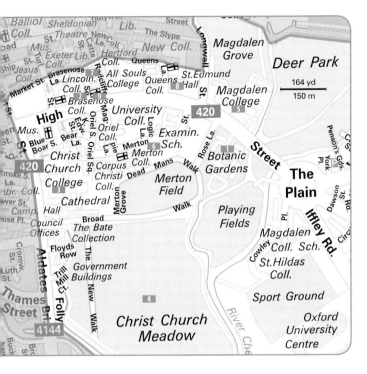

SIGHTSEEING IN THE OLD TOWN: UP AND DOWN HIGH STREET

1 Botanic Garden
2 Brasenose College
3 Christ Church
4 Christ Church Meadow
5 Magdalen College

6 Merton College
7 Radcliffe Camera
8 St Edmund Hall
9 University Church of St Mary the Virgin

4 CHRIST CHURCH MEADOW ☆
(122 B–C 4–5) (*M* F–G7)

From the ● southern end, this large meadow between Isis and Cherwell offers fabulous views of the *dreaming spires*. To the south, a pretty bridge leads to the triangular island with the college boathouses. The centre of the meadow is often flooded, or being grazed by rare Longhorn cattle (don't worry, there is a fence!). Keep a look out for the historic spoilsport signs tell-

ing you all the things that you aren't allowed to do on the meadow, such as fly kites, throw stones, do cartwheels, and shoot arrows or pistols. It's not fair – you're not allowed to do anything!
An idyllic stroll around the Meadow takes you along New Walk, the Isis and the Cherwell, then on to Dead Man's Walk (this was where the dead were carried to the Jewish cemetery in the Middle Ages), and back along Broad Walk. A memorial on Dead Man's Walk

Venerable Magdalen College Chapel is also home to various curiosities

commemorates the balloon pioneer James Sadler, who amazed the world from this Oxford meadow. *Early in the morning (because of the rowers!) until nightfall | Entrances St Aldate's/through Christ Church War Memorial Gardens, Merton Grove, Rose Lane, and the revolving door behind the Head of the River pub | short.travel/oxf17*

5 MAGDALEN COLLEGE ★
(122 C3) (*ØØ G6*)

How about a Bambi burger? Don't worry – it's not really on the menu. But there are deer here – obtained in the 17th century as a source of food, they graze either in the Grove or on the *Water Meadow*. Stroll over the idyllic circular path called *Addison's Walk*. Wherever you happen to be on Magdalen's (pronounced Mawdlin's) expansive land, the college (found-

ed in 1458) delights with its charming atmosphere.

And if you're on the lookout for the grotesque gargoyles, you'll find plenty here! In *St John's Quad* you'll see an ancient open-air stone pulpit that is used on St John's Day (24 June). The heart of the college is *Cloister Quad*, which dates back to the 15th century and has a medieval flair – apart from the bright red retro telephone box! Something else you'll see here, as is the case in many of the colleges, are the commemorative boards to students who fell in the two World Wars. In the antechamber to the *Chapel* is a copy of Leonardo da Vinci's "Last Supper", and there's also a secret under the choir stalls: *misericords* are (often indecent) wood carvings that the choristers could secretly lean against.

The Classic *New Building* was new in the 18th century, and was intended to be the start of a vast new *quad* – but as you can see, it came to nothing, and here it stands, alone and abandoned in the large green meadow. The *Bell Tower* of 1509 is famous mainly for its role in the May Day ritual (page 100).

A quiet spot with views of Magdalen Bridge and the punts on the Cherwell is the garden of the *Old Kitchen Bar* – you can still see the original 13th century fireplaces. *Jan–Jun and Oct–Dec 1pm–6pm, end Jun–early Sep 10am–7pm, Sep noon–7pm | High Street | £6 | www.magd.ox.ac.uk*

⑥ MERTON COLLEGE
(122 B3–4) (*𝄞 F6–7*)

Merton likes to be described in superlatives: the oldest college, the cleverest students. It's certainly super-old: it was founded in 1264! The medieval library is INSIDER TIP the only college library in Oxford that you can visit *(only as part of a tour of the college | Jul–Sep 2pm and 3pm | £5 | Book at the Porter's Lodge or at tours@merton.ox.ac.uk)*. It's well worth visiting – and it's tremendous fun to shuffle in felt slippers between the venerable ancient books, some of them secured by chains.

As is customary in Oxford, the two medieval quads *Mob Quad* and *Front Quad* argue about which of them is older. A strange ritual takes place in *Fellow's Quad* every autumn between 2 and 3 in the morning when the clocks go back after summer time: dressed in their academic gowns, the Mertonians link arms and, drinking port, march backwards. Another of Merton's curiosities is one of the few Real Tennis courts left in England (page 25). *Mon–Fri 2pm–5pm, Sat/Sun 10am–5pm | £3 | Merton Street | www.merton.ox.ac.uk*

⑦ RADCLIFFE CAMERA ★
(122 B3) (*𝄞 F6*)

A round building on a square? *Why not!* This circular library was founded in 1749, and today is the most famous building in Oxford. VIP doctor John Radcliffe not only left the university his private library, but also money to build the "Rad Cam", which nowadays is used as a reading room. It looks most impressive from the outside, but if you would like to see the inside, you can do so on a 90-minute Bodleian Library Tour. *Guided tour £14 | Tour upstairs/downstairs Wed/Sat 9.15am, or Explore the Reading Rooms tour Sun 11.15am and 1.15pm | Radcliffe Square | tel. 01865 287400 | short.travel/oxf3*

⑧ ST EDMUND HALL
(122 C3) (*𝄞 G6*)

Although these 13th century student halls and teaching facility only officially became a college in 1957, it is the oldest educational establishment in Oxford. The charming little *Front Quad* is one of the most attractive college quads of them all. Be sure to visit "Teddy Hall", not least for the church *St Peter in the East*, which has a hidden INSIDER TIP crypt underneath it. The church itself dates back to the 12th century, and has been a college library since 1970. Little has changed in the gloomy crypt in the last 1,000 years – but it's still sinister: it contains a random hotchpotch of heavy stone-carved gravestones! Grave robbers at work? No – the things are made of polystyrene! Backdrop for the detective series "Lewis". If you want to visit the crypt, you need to make an appointment with the bursar *(tel. 01865 279005 | bursary@seh.ox.ac.uk)*. *Daily 10am–4pm | admission free | Queen's Lane | www.seh.ox.ac.uk*

9 UNIVERSITY CHURCH OF
ST MARY THE VIRGIN ★ ☼
(122 B3) (*🕮 F6*)

Oxford, *"City of the dreaming spires"* – so it stands to reason that there should be lots of fabulous lookout points. However, quite literally nothing can top the Gothic tower of 13th century St Mary's! It's narrow at the top, which is why you may sometimes see a sign saying, *"Tower full, wait in line"* at the entrance. But your reward after the exciting climb up 127 steps of the steep winding staircase are the most breathtaking views! Next to St Mary's is today's *Vaults & Garden Café* (page 52), which for centuries was where the first university meetings and exams were held until a new home was found for them in 1534 in the Divinity School.

Tea for two (or more) at the Vaults & Garden Café

Incidentally, Mahatma Gandhi was also at Oxford... for a weekend in 1931. Here in St Mary's, a hidden INSIDER TIP mini Gandhi is a memorial to his visit: look for a bony figure clad in a loincloth and sitting in the lotus position at the western end of the ceiling (above the window with views of Radcliffe Camera). *Entrances on High Street and Radcliffe Square | Church Mon–Sat 9am–6pm, Sun noon–6pm | admission free, tower Mon–Sat 9.30am–6pm, Sun 11.30am–6pm | £4 | www.university-church.ox.ac.uk*

OLD TOWN: EAST OF ST GILES

A real treat for those with a thirst for knowledge: the north-eastern end of High Street is full of historic colleges, libraries and museums. And after all that education, rest your legs in the relaxing *University Parks* (always plural) which at the north-eastern end stretch as far as the pretty River Cherwell.

10 BODLEIAN LIBRARY
(122 B3) (*🕮 F6*)

The Bodleian houses over 12 million books on a total of 370 km/230 mi of shelves, many of them in the venerable library itself, but most in underground tunnels and external warehouses. The library is named after Thomas Bodley, who knocked the rundown building and collection of medieval books into shape in the 17th century. In 1610 he negotiated the deal whereby one issue of every single book published in the UK had to be deposited in his library – and that is still the case today. Bodley also made the rule that none of the books could be

SIGHTSEEING

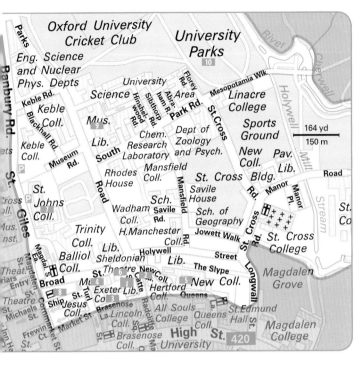

SIGHTSEEING IN THE OLD TOWN: EAST OF ST GILES

1. Bodleian Library
2. Bridge of Sighs
3. Exeter College
4. Museum of the History of Science
5. New College
6. Sheldonian Theatre
7. St John's College
8. St Michael at the North Gate
9. UMNH & Pitt Rivers Museum
10. University Parks

lent to readers. There are no exceptions. In 1645, even King Charles I was refused permission after giving the pompous order that he should be brought a book. No exceptions. *Rules are rules!*

The heart of the Bodleian is the *Old Schools Quad*. The best bit about it: the *Tower of the Five Orders* (1613–24). From the bottom of the building to the top it stands like a vast stone crib sheet and displays the columns of the five orders

of classical architecture: Tuscan, Doric, Ionic, Corinthian and the Composite order. Worth knowing! Opposite the tower you will see the *Divinity School* (1420–88, *admission without tour £1*). Not so much to look at on the outside, but inside… pure Gothic! The ceiling is decorated in the Perpendicular style with figures, symbols and the initials of sponsors. You don't need a ticket for the Proscholium (entrance) – sometimes the door to the

Divinity School is ajar, and you can have a quick look inside.

If you want to see a few books as well as the architecture, go online or to the ticket office to book one of the various ● guided tours *(short.travel/oxf6)*, e.g. 30/60/90 minutes for £6/8/14. The mini tour will also take you through the medieval *Duke Humfrey's Library*. For Harry Potter fans: the sanatorium scenes in the films were shot at the Divinity School, and Duke Humfrey's provided the backdrop for the Hogwarts library. Audio guides (£2.50) cover the *quads* and Divinity School. Tip for social media addicts: there are INSIDER TIP▶ particularly cool Snapchat filters here! *Mon–Fri 9am–5pm, Sat 9am–4.30pm, Sun 11am–5pm | Great Gate, Catte Street | tel. 01865 277000 | www.bodleian.ox.ac.uk*

From Oxford's loveliest building to its ugliest (according to some people): critics shrieked indignantly in 1946 that the newly-opened *New Bodleian Library* on the other side of Broad Street looked like a swimming pool! After an extensive conversion in 2015, it reinvented itself as the *Weston Library* – and it's well worth popping in to see the (free) exhibitions of the treasures in the university library. The *Bodleian Café* in the atrium of the large Blackwell Hall with views of the "ancient tomes" high up behind state-of-the-art glass and steel is one of Oxford's coolest addresses for brunch *(Mon–Fri 8.30am–4.30pm, Sat 9am–4.30pm, Sun 11am–4.30pm | Weston Library, Broad Street | tel. 01865 277248 | short.travel/oxf7)*

Star architect Nicholas Hawksmoor built the *Clarendon Building (Broad Street)* in 1715, which once upon a time was part of the Bodleian. You can see nine lovely ladies right on the top: the three muses who inspire the arts.

⓫ BRIDGE OF SIGHS ★
(122 B3) (*⌀ F6*)

The covered Bridge of Sighs is officially (but far more boringly) called Hertford Bridge, and joins two sections of Hertford College. Founded in 1282 as Hart Hall, the college almost had to close in 1814, when it had only one student! However, it survived, and in 1913 the Bridge of Sighs (based on the eponymous bridge in Venice) was built as a skyway over New College Lane to join two *quads*. Smart alecks like to announce at this point that the bridge looks more like the Rialto Bridge in Venice. There's only one response: sigh! *New College Lane / near Catte Street*

⓬ EXETER COLLEGE ⚜
(122 B3) (*⌀ F6*)

Relatively small Exeter College, founded in 1314, has the INSIDER TIP▶ best place for a selfie in all Oxford! In the Front Quad, walk through the door marked "Fellows' Garden" on the opposite side. From the wall at the top, you will have a breathtaking view of nearby Radcliffe Camera. And while you're here, have a look at the large, neo-Gothic chapel by Gilbert Scott, complete with a wall hanging by William Morris (the artist, not the industrialist) and Edward Burne-Jones. There is another art treasure that you can only see from the outside on Broad Street: what's that – a naked man on the roof?! No. The oversized iron sculpture by sculptor Anthony Gormley. *Daily 2pm–5pm | admission free | Turl Street | tel. 01865 279600 | www.exeter.ox.ac.uk*

Exeter College is the *alma mater* of "Lord of the Rings" author J.R.R. Tolkien, later (together with fantasy and professorial colleague C.S. Lewis) a long-time member of the writers' table at the Eagle and Child. A place of pilgrimage for fans of the Middle Earth: INSIDER TIP▶ Tolkien's grave in the cemetery of the nearby village of Wolvercote.

13 MUSEUM OF THE HISTORY OF SCIENCE (122 B3) (*Ⓜ F6*)

Wow – the oldest university museum in the world! Even though it may stand in the shadow of the Sheldonian Theatre, the building from 1683 is an eye-catcher. Today at the Museum of the History of

family trails (free), see website for regular programme changes | Broad Street | tel. 01865 277280 | www.mhs.ox.ac.uk | Pocket Curator Museum App (free)

14 NEW COLLEGE ● (122 B–C3) (*Ⓜ F–G6*)

"New College"?! Well, it might have been 600 years ago! The idea of grouping all the main buildings around a *front quad*

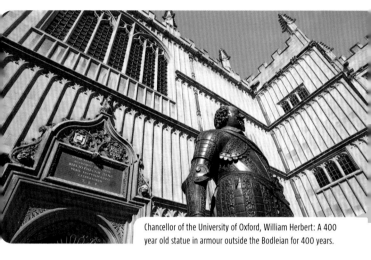

Chancellor of the University of Oxford, William Herbert: A 400 year old statue in armour outside the Bodleian for 400 years.

Science, you can admire amazing instruments from the Middle Ages to the 19th century, including various surreal but functional quadrants, astrolabes, sundials and early mathematical instruments, an anatomical model of a hand from the 16th century, Lewis Carroll's camera, the first penicillin, made in bed pans and biscuit tins, and countless other curiosities. In the basement is a INSIDER TIP blackboard used by Albert Einstein during a lecture in Oxford in 1931. Hint for finding the Einstein formula: L.J. stands for *light years*! Tue–Sun noon–5pm | admission free | Museum Highlights Tour (free) Thu 2.30pm, 3.15pm, Sat 12.30pm, 1.15pm |

was tried for the first time at New College. Its success was so great that you can now see the same arrangement in most of the later colleges.

The strange objects that have been collected in New College over the centuries are said to include two unicorns – although scientists concluded that the bony poking things are in fact narwhal tusks. Shame! The 14th century cloister houses spooky, dark tomb slabs that are kept company by discarded crumbling figures of saints from St Mary's Church. There is a holm oak in the Cloister Quad that is a film star – it was featured in one of the Harry Potter films.

There is much to see and admire in the *chapel*. In the *ante chapel* is an Eric Gill INSIDER TIP memorial plaque which lists 263 names of students who fell in WWI. Other art treasures in the chapel are the west window by Joshua Reynolds, and directly beneath that the unsettling statue of Lazarus by Jacob Epstein and, in the vestry, a painting by El Greco.

The boundary on the north side of the garden is the original town wall from the 12th century. Back then, this area was used partly as the municipal rubbish dump, and partly as a mass grave for victims of the plague. In the sunken garden is a lookout mound that dates back to the 17th century. According to one rumour, it is said to squeak if you clap your hands. Well? Does it? Try it at your own risk – but observe the signs: *"Don't walk on the grass!" mid Oct–mid Mar 2pm–4pm, admission free, mid Mar–mid Oct 11am–5pm, £4 | Entrance mid Oct–mid Mar Holywell Street, mid Mar–mid Oct at the end of New College Lane | www.new.ox.ac.uk*

15 SHELDONIAN THEATRE ★
(122 B3) (*F6*)

One of the first buildings (1664–69) by the architect Sir Christopher Wren. Nothing like this had ever been seen before! The circular Sheldonian looks a little bit like a Roman amphitheatre, but with a roof?! Yes – you need a roof in rainy Oxford. And Wren's roof really is in a league of its own. With no irritating columns to disturb the view, it balances, floats elegantly, and with magnificent paintings on the outside, on the circular base – a sensation of early Modernism. But once again, things are not quite what they seem: the Sheldonian isn't in fact a theatre, but primarily the university ceremony hall. Today it is also the venue for first-class concerts (*short.*

travel/oxf18) in a wonderful setting that helps you to forget (if you opt for one of the cheaper seats) that the knees of the person behind you are digging into your back. ⚘ Fabulous views of the medieval old town from the glazed octagonal cupola. *Feb–Apr Mon–Sat 10am–4.30pm, May–Sep daily 10am–4.30pm, Oct Mon–Sat 10am–4.30pm, Nov–Jan Mon–Sat 10am–3pm | Broad Street | £3.50 | 1-hour guided tour May–Sep £8 | tel. 01865 277299 | short.travel/oxf9*

Surrounding the Sheldonian Theatre on plinths are 13 stoical characters called the *Emperors' Heads*. Only the emperors... well, they aren't! But it was Max Beerbohm who referred to them as such in his satirical novel "Zuleika Dobson" (1911), and the name has stuck. It is highly likely that the head-and-shoulder busts of 1669 (the current ones are in fact the third set) are not actually of anyone specific, and certainly not of any emperors. The poor fellows have had to put up with quite a bit over the years: students regularly derive a tremendous amount of pleasure from adorning them with traffic cones and applying lipstick to them.

16 ST JOHN'S COLLEGE
(122 A–B2) (*F5–6*)

In 1555, a wealthy merchant, Sir Thomas White, founded a new college in buildings that had belonged to the former College of St Bernard, a monastery of the Cistercian order (1437). St John: the patron saint of merchants (and priests and teachers, but that's not relevant here). So the name makes sense. St John's is one of the loveliest and wealthiest colleges in Oxford. It owns so much land that it is said you can go all the way to Cambridge without leaving its land. And what do you do when there's enough money left over? That's right – you rebuild! St John's is a permanent

The ceiling painting in the Sheldonian Theatre is well worth the crick in your neck

building site. The new library is due for completion in the summer of 2018, and sadly the vast, beautiful, listed garden is closed for the duration of the work. St John's is of particular interest for its many extensions: you'll find architectural styles ranging from the Middle Ages to the very latest in Post-Modernism integrated in daily college life. The statue of St Bernard above the entrance is a testimony to the college's origins, and on the inside is a far more modern St John by Eric Gill (1936). On the right in the passage from the Front Quad to the North Quad is the entrance to the chapel of 1530, which was left over from the Cistercian monastery. The *Beehive* in the North Quad does not have any bees in it, but is a complex of non-regular hexagonal rooms from the 1960s. A bronze replica of a married couple has stood gazing at the grass in the magnificent Canterbury Quad for almost 400 years: to the east

is King Charles I, and to the west his wife, Queen Henrietta Maria. Both appeared in person in 1636 as top VIPS at the magnificent inauguration of the quad – which cost more than the actual building did! *Daily from 1pm–5pm | admission free | St Giles | www.sjc.ox.ac.uk*

17 ST MICHAEL AT THE NORTH GATE ☼ (122 A–B3) (*ω F6*)
It's hard to imagine how old St Michael is: the chunky tower in the middle of the city is Oxford's oldest building. In 1040 it helped the Anglo Saxons look out for their enemies, the Danes. Half way up, you can admire the ancient mechanical movement in action, as well as a curious collection of antiquities: amidst the faded documents, tarnished coins and massive iron keys, you'll also find some 17th century hair curlers and a Sheela-na-gig – a figurative carving of a naked woman with an exaggerated vulva, dating back

to the 11th century. Climb the 97 steps up the tower, and enjoy the first-class views over Oxford from the airy roof.

Inside the church, there are stained glass windows from the 13th century and a baptismal font that was installed later and over which one Uncle William once held his godchild, the son of an Oxford landlord, in 1606. Uncle William's surname? Shakespeare!

Summer 10.30am–5pm, winter 10.30am–4.30pm | £2.50 | Cornmarket Street / corner Ship Street | www.smng.org.uk/wp

18 UNIVERSITY MUSEUM OF NATURAL HISTORY ★ & PITT RIVERS MUSEUM (122 B1–2) (*ØØ F5*)

Who walked over the grass outside the museum? It was the prehistoric megalosaurus, whose footprints were taken from a stone quarry near Oxford, and makes people want to visit the Museum of Natural History. You think the Gothic building looks more like a church? It does

– it was finished in 1860, and many small-minded Victorians wrinkled their noses indignantly at the sight of the new "Cathedral to science". So admire the actual building at least as much as you would the inside – it's worth a visit just to see the impressive main hall with a delicate glass roof. The windows at the front show you where the money ran out for the construction – some are decorated on all sides with ornate exotic plants, birds and animals, and some are not. In addition to the spectacular dinosaur skeletons, the UMNH is also home to a few sad remains from the unofficial symbol of Oxford: the unfortunate dodo, which became extinct in the 17th century, and was a quaint flightless bird that found fame in Lewis Carroll's "Alice in Wonderland". Living birds can be seen on the roof of the museum tower: in the summer months, you can watch nesting swifts up close thanks to the webcam *(www.oum. ox.ac.uk/swifts.htm)*. Other living "ex-

Plenty of bones, nothing broken: dinosaur skeletons at the Museum of Natural History

hibits" include hissing cockroaches and a swarm of bees in the Upper Gallery. Head for the new *Museum café* to relax over a refreshing cup of tea and look at the dinos. Don't miss this on the steps: an oversized (abandoned!) nest of the "European" or "German" wasp, Vespula Germanica.

Daily 10am–5pm | Sun 2pm–4pm Family-friendly Sundays (no need to book) | Talks, workshops, special events: go to "What's on" on the museum website | admission free | Parks Road | www.oum.ox.ac.uk

Look out! A lot of people go straight past it: an unassuming archway in the farthest corner of the UMNH leads to the ● *Pitt Rivers Museum*. This full-to-bursting, rather dark iconic museum makes little sense – but is tremendous fun: an ex-General and amateur Indiana Jones, Augustus Pitt Rivers collected vast quantities of old things, sexy feathered garments, seal intestines, ancient tattoo equipment, a witch in a bottle, shrunken heads and other off-the-wall stuff from everywhere and nowhere. Oh, and here's something else: that thing that you can see sticking out of the INSIDER TIP mummy's bandages and looks like a prune is, in fact, a shrivelled toe. You might want to wait a while before you have some plum tart in the cafeteria! Go to *www.prm.ox.ac.uk/whatson* for a changing programme with eccentric talks, workshops and late-night events at the museum. *Mon noon–4.30pm, Tue–Sun 10am–4.30pm | admission free | short.travel/oxf8*

19 UNIVERSITY PARKS ★
(122 A–C1) (*Ø F–G 4–5*)

And… breathe! The green haven west of the River Cherwell is for everyone, not just academics. But the university has looked after the Parks (always with an 's' – why?) no one knows!) and its more than 1,600 trees, rare plants, sports

fields, walks and art installations since 1860. Don't miss this opportunity to watch some really INSIDER TIP first-class cricket *(free; dates at www.cricketintheparks.org.uk)*. And when it's time for a break, settle yourself on the *Tolkien bench* or ● *Havel's Place* beside the idyllic pond – it's a usable work of art with a table and two chairs that is a memorial to the late writer and former Czech president, Václav Havel. A quiet path leads through *Mesopotamia* – the small plot of land between the two arms of the Cherwell. "Parson's Pleasure", the (in)famous male-only nude bathing area, was at the south end of the park until 1991. Sounds like fun – but what about a similar area for female bathers? There was – although it was closed in 1970, but its name was just as appealing as that of its male counterpart: "Dame's Delight".

Daily 7.45am until dusk (the Mesopotamia Walk closes 30 min earlier) | admission free | Parks Road | www.parks.ox.ac.uk/home | If you get locked in: tel. 01865 272944

FROM THE CASTLE DISTRICT TO JERICHO

Oxford is split in half by Banbury Road to the north and Abingdon Road to the south. The brewing and working-class district – and a number of ugly 1960s concrete blocks – used to be west of the merging St Giles, Magdalen Street, Cornmarket Street and St Aldate's. Much has been, and is still being modernised today, after the castle quarter and Westgate shopping mall, the railway station has also been given a makeover. Between the canal and Banbury Road lie Walton Street, Little Clarendon Street (good for window shopping and entertainment) and the extremely popular quarter of Jericho with its boutiques, cafés, restaurants and cool bars.

20 ASHMOLEAN MUSEUM ★
(122 A2) (∅ E–F6)

The art and archaeology museum started as a collection of curiosities in the back room of a London pub in the early 17th century. At home in the purpose-built, pompously classical columned building, and extensively modernised for a large amount of money in 2009,

Apples, pears and more:
the Veg Van also stops in Jericho

The Veg Van

the Ashmolean offers an attractive and versatile programme of permanent and special exhibitions and events that are not just for culture vultures *(www.ashmolean.org/events)*. These are the top highlights you absolutely should not miss: Level 2, Gallery 41: King Alfred Jewel – a 9th century reading aid (not glasses, but an embellishment for a kind of manuscript pointer), Level 1, Gallery 8: Powhatan's Mantle – embroidered chief's cloak that belonged to Pocahontas' father, c. 1600, and: Guy Fawkes' lantern – that is said to have belonged to the early-modern British would-be bomber. Even lots of Oxfordians are unaware that you can come here and admire ● valuable works by Michelangelo and Raphael from up close: email *waprintroom@ashmus.ox.ac.uk* (at least a day in advance) for an appointment. A word of warning for visitors with lacquered nails: you will be given special protective gloves.

You can then recover from all this art and culture above Oxford's dreaming spires in the rooftop restaurant INSIDER TIP *Benugo (Tue, Wed, Sun 10am–4.30pm, Thu–Sat 10am–10pm (after 5pm entrance through St Giles) | Live music from 7pm in summer | tel. 01865 553823 | www.benu go.com/restaurants/rooftop-restaurant).*
Tue–Sun 10am–5pm | Programme of daily (free) guided tours at short. travel/oxf10 | Beaumont Street | tel. 01865 278000 | www.ashmolean.org

21 BLAVATNIK SCHOOL OF GOVERN-MENT (121 F1–2) (∅ E5)

Oxford has its own UFO! No; this flying saucer made of glass, steel and solid wood is the latest construction by the Swiss star architects Herzog & de Meuron, and since 2016 has been home to the university department sponsored

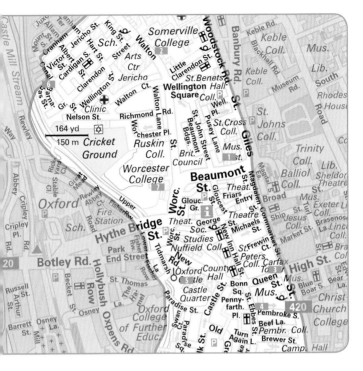

SIGHTSEEING FROM THE CASTLE DISTRICT TO JERICHO

1 Ashmolean Museum
2 Blavatnik School of Government
3 Carfax Tower
4 Modern Art Oxford
5 Oxford Castle
6 St Barnabas Church
7 Worcester College

by the Ukrainian oligarch Len Blavatnik. Whatever you think of this unmissable, glittering behemoth in the midst of all the traditional, classic, medieval buildings in Oxford, you really have to see it! It's actually enough to do so from the outside, but if you INSIDER TIP book an event (often free), you can also admire the School of Government from the inside *(www.bsg.ox.ac.uk/events)*. There are three Open Days a year. *Walton Street | tel. 01865 614343 | www.bsg.ox.ac.uk*

🔆 CARFAX TOWER 🔆
(122 A–B3) (ⓜ F6)

Carfax: the historic junction in the city centre where the roads from all four directions met in the dim and distant past. Carfax Tower is all that remains of the 12th century St. Martin's Church – the main part of it was demolished in the 19th century because it was deemed to be in the way. A few weathered, medieval tombstones can still be seen on the ground. There are fabulous panoramic views from the square tower (up 99 narrow steps). Contrary to expectations, you will have to wait a long time to hear the *quarterboys* on the outside of the tower hammer on the bells for all they're worth: although it does chime every quarter-hour, it does so without any visible help. Carfax is also where the infamous Swyndlestock Tavern (page 14) once stood. *Daily Apr–Oct 10am–5.30pm, Nov–Mar 10am–3pm | £2.20 | Carfax, corner Queen Street/Cornmarket Street*

23 MODERN ART OXFORD
(122 A5–6) (*F6*)

The Museum of Modern Art makes sure that Oxford is famous for new things as well as old. Changing, high-calibre exhibitions have been taking place in the white-painted halls of the former brewery since 1965 by artists including Joseph Beuys, Yoko Ono, Tracey Emin and the Chapman Brothers. Fiona Cullinane and Lorraine Wood will treat you to a good brunch, lunch or afternoon refreshment in the indus-trial-chic setting of *St Ebbe's Kitchen (Tue–Sat 10am–5pm, Sun noon–5pm | tel. 01865 201491 | Moderate). Tue–Sun 11am–6pm, Sun noon–5pm | admission free | 30 Pembroke Street | www.mod ernartoxford.org.uk*

24 OXFORD CASTLE ★
(122 A3) (*E6*)

The oldest part of Oxford, and at the same time the newest: the rather shabby and run-down *Castle Quarter* has been completely refurbished in recent years, and now boasts various chic eateries, a boutique hotel and sheltered spots for markets and open-air theatre performances *(www. oxfordcastlequarter.com)*. Its roots go back almost 1,000 years: in 1071, the Norman baron Robert D'Oilly had an impressive moated castle built; today, all that remain are the *mound* and *St George's Tower*. Most of the time the castle was used as a prison, and in fact the last jailbirds were only released in 1996. Thousands had been imprisoned here under appalling conditions – including lazy and rebellious students in the Middle Ages! Book the 40-minute "Oxford Castle Unlocked" tour, and il-lustrious, costumed figures from the past will take you through St George's Tower, the Victorian jail and the spooky crypt with much drama and élan. In the Middle Ages, the crypt was also used as a cooling chamber for food – and dead bodies. After the tour, you can visit an interesting and somewhat grizzly exhi-bition on the history of the jail castle. *Daily from 10am, last tour at 4.20pm |*

LOW BUDGET

The Bate Collection of Musical Instruments **(122 B4)** (*F7*), which belongs to the university's music faculty, contains historic musical instruments from the Middle Ages to the modern era. Friendly music students will help you produce a sound from strangely shaped instruments in the Handling Collection *(Mon–Fri 2pm–5pm, also Sat 10am–noon during term time | admission free | St Aldate's | tel. 01865 276139 | www.bate.ox.ac.uk)*.

University Open Days take place every year in June and September, and are a wonderful opportunity to explore the colleges and courses free of charge *(short.travel/oxf2)*.

£10.95 | New Road | www.oxfordcastle unlocked.co.uk

25 ST BARNABAS CHURCH
(121 E2) (*D–E5*)

If you take the train heading north, you get as far as Jericho in a couple of minutes, and could easily think you had accidentally travelled to Italy: it's a genuine Campanile! In fact, the neo-Romanesque church with the bell tower which is visible from afar was based on an original in Torcello in Venice. A Byzantine basilica: this No-Man's-Land between Walton Street and the railway line really is a surprising sight, and a refreshing contrast to the rest of the city's architecture. Take a few minutes to relax in this unexpectedly special oasis of peace. St Barnabas is often open during the day; you will find the current events on the website. *Fri/Tue morning and for services | St Barnabas Street | stbarnabasoxford@gmail.com | www.sbarnabas.org.uk*

26 WORCESTER COLLEGE ●
(121 F2–3) (*E6*)

Clever Oxford professors made this college famous with their invention of the eponymous sauce. Right? Wrong! Worcester was named by its founder in the area around the city of Worcester in 1714. Before that, there was already a college with a similar name here in the 13th century: *Gloucester*. The pretty cottages to the left of the Main Quad are all that remain today. Past the cottage, turn left down a narrow passageway, and on the right you'll see an enchanted garden with overgrown arches, mythical beasts on stone benches and weeping willow branches drooping over the pond. This is Lewis Carroll's "Pool of Tears" that was immortalised in "Alice in Wonderland". In the *chapel*, the Vic-

torian eccentric William Burges covered every square millimetre with unusual mosaics, paintings, glass birds and animals. *Daily 2pm–7pm | admission free | Walton Street | www.worc.ox.ac.uk*

You'll have the city at your feet from Carfax Tower

ALSO WORTH SEEING

COWLEY ROAD ●
(123 D–F 4–6) (*H–K 7–8*)

Cowley Road is a relatively tourist-free zone – yet this road in the east offers a fascinating mix of a young, international atmosphere and history's forgotten secrets. If you'd like to see a shrivelled piece of skin that – allegedly – is from none other than the Apostle Bartholomew, you can do so in *St Bartholomew's Chapel*, a relic from a 14th century leper colony. There is a stone maze with Celtic-like symbols at the church of *St Mary & St John* – under your feet are the mortal remains of the poorest of the poor – inmates of the former Victorian *workhouse*. A very special INSIDER TIP quiz is hidden in the pavements: look for 28 pairs of round bronze plaques hidden between the roundabout at The Plain and Magdalen Road – all with typical East Oxford themes.

Thirsty and hungry? You'll find the most exotic and best value cafés, bars and restaurants in Oxford here.

HEADINGTON SHARK (O) *(🕮 O)*

Look out – there's a shark on the roof! Is it raining monsters?! No – it's modern art: in 1986, radio broadcaster Bill Heine installed the 7.6 metre/25 ft long piscine sculpture on his otherwise completely unassuming terraced house in Headington. The unconventional work of art by John Buckley was intended as a protest against the nuclear attacks and accidents of the 1980s. The neighbours shook their heads; the council wanted to see the (non-existent, of course) planning permission for a shark-on-roof installation, and everyone else stood on the street and looked, thought it was great fun, and took photographs. Since then, Bill has written a book ("The Hunting of the Shark"), and the shark has its own Facebook page. *2 New High Street | Headington*

MINI PLANT OXFORD (O) *(🕮 O)*

Oxford has been closely linked to the automotive industry ever since William Morris, later Lord Nuffield, opened his first bicycle and automobile workshop on Longwall Street in 1912. Morris Garages produced the MG and other cars, and today the former Morris Motors company in Cowley belongs to BMW and produces the Mini models Hatch/Hardtop, Clubman, Convertible, Coupé and Roadster. Guided tours of the factory are extremely popular with Mini and Maxi fans (from 14 years of age)! Book in advance, either online or by phone; times are available on the website. *Mon–Tue 9am–6pm, Fri 9am–1pm | £19 | Eastern Bypass Road | tel. 01865 825750 | www.visit-mini.com/ visitmini | Bus no. 10 to Horspath Road Turning Circle stop*

PORT MEADOW ●
(116–117 A–E 1–6) *(🕮 B–D 1–4)*

Just a short walk from the city centre, to the north-west, you'll come across an incredible natural oasis that has remained untouched for thousands of years. Expansive landscapes and the company of wild birds and flowers, cattle and horses as you run, walk, fly a kite or picnic – it's hard to believe that you're so close to the city. You can relax after your walk at one of the two traditional pubs, *The Perch* (p. 59) and *The Trout Inn* (p. 59). It might get muddy when it rains, so it's a good idea to take your wellies! *Free access | Entrances Walton Well Road and Aristotle Lane to the south, Godstow/Wolvercote to the north | short.travel/oxf11*

ST FRIDESWIDE'S CHURCH
(121 E3) *(🕮 D6)*

This small, unassuming church on Osney Island is rarely open, but holds a secret that is well worth seeing: INSIDER TIP a door that was carved by Alice Liddell, the inspiration behind the fictional Alice in Wonderland. The panelling from

The gardens of Worcester College inspired Lewis Carroll

1880 shows St Frideswide travelling in a boat from Binsey to Oxford. Both the saint and Alice herself undertook this boat trip (see St Margaret of Antioch). You'll find the door leaning in a corner to the left of the pulpit. *Sun (before and after the service) 9.45am–10.30am and 11.30am–noon, Wed (before Evening Prayer) 4.45pm | Botley Road, opposite Botley Park / West Oxford Community Centre | short.travel/oxf12*

ST MARGARET OF ANTIOCH AND TREACLE WELL (116 B5) (*B3*)

Not far to the north-west is the pretty little village of Binsey, and a 10-minute walk away is the small medieval church of St Margaret of Antioch (often surrounded by cute pygmy goats). Don't be shy about having a look at the front right of the pulpit: on the inside, the wood carving of Maggie faces the preacher's legs — possibly so that the saint, depicted with such a passion for detail, doesn't distract the good worshippers from the sermon? Just around the corner is the ancient *Treacle Well* – a portal to the underworld! But it doesn't really have anything to do with treacle: the word comes from the Middle English word *triacle*, which means holy water. St Frideswide (p. 13) is said to have caused the healing spring to appear. Church and spring: now secret tips, but in the Middle Ages absolute magnets for pilgrims. Lewis Carroll and Alice Liddell visited the spring on a boat trip on the Isis - and it's now immortalised in "Alice in Wonderland". *Binsey Lane, Binsey | www.osney-benefice.org.uk/node/4*

Stratford-upon-Avon: the name of the town's great son is everywhere

OUTSIDE THE CITY

BLENHEIM PALACE (O) (🗺 O)

This stunning estate lies 13 km/8.1 mi north of Oxford in the picturesque village of Woodstock. It takes a good half-hour to get there on the S3 bus line *(www.stagecoachbus.com)*. The baroque palace was named after the little village of Blindheim on the Danube, where in 1704 the Duke of Marlborough defeated the French and the Bavarians. Designed by John Vanbrugh and built in 1722 by Nicholas Hawksmoor, the palace looks like something designed for Hollywood, a highly dramatic film backdrop, but is in fact still home to the Marlborough family – which included Winston Churchill, who was born here in 1874.

The *buggy tour (£4 | 25 min)* is fun: you ride through the wonderful park and around the lake on a kind of golf buggy, and are given a running commentary. There are daily guided tours of the spectacular gardens (included in the price of the ticket) at 12.30pm, depending on the weather. Afterwards, head to one of the palace's cafés or restaurants for some refreshments. Don't miss: Afternoon Tea in the *Orangery (weekends only, noon–5pm, book in advance on the website under "Book a table").*

Daily 10.30am–5.30pm | Palace, park and garden £24.90 | Woodstock | www. blenheimpalace.com
In the village itself, the *Woodstock Arms (daily from 7.30am | 6–8 Market Street | tel. 01993 811251 | www.thewoodstock arms.com | Moderate)* is a country pub that offers good food, a friendly, cosy atmosphere and comfortable rooms. Next door, **INSIDER TIP** a secret tip for gin fans: in the *Courtyard Bar* of the Feathers Hotel, choose from over 400 (!) different types of gin.

STRATFORD-UPON-AVON (0) (*↷ 0*)
Shakespeare's town, 65 km/40.4 mi north-west of Oxford. A National Express coach will get you there in an hour. The main attractions are the five *Shakespeare Houses*: Birthplace, New Place, Hall's Croft, Anne Hathaway's Cottage and Mary Arden's Farm. *The houses all have different opening times, but usually in winter they are daily from 10am–4pm, spring–autumn daily from 9am–5pm | Ticket for all five houses £26.25, available from all the houses, other ticket combinations possible | www.shakespeare.org. uk/visit*
The *Visitor Centre* can help you arrange tickets, accommodation and other bookings, and you can download a map of the town from the website *(Mon–Sat 9am–5.30pm, Sun 10am–4pm | Bridgeway | tel. 01789 264293 | www.discover-stratford. com)*. Tickets for the well-known *Royal Shakespeare Company* are extremely popular – book in advance *(tel. 01789 403493 | www.rsc.org.uk)*! After the performance, head for the cosy *Dirty Duck (Waterside | tel. 01789 297312 | Budget)* and raise a glass with the actors.

FIT IN THE CITY

They glide over the water silently and elegantly – the gondolas of Venice. The Oxford version is different:
★ ● *Punting* means fun, plenty of fun, and plenty of noisy fun! Of course, you can hire a "gondolier" to do the work for you, but it's much more fun to do it yourself! In brief, this is how it works: hire your punt and stick the pole in the river. The boat will shoot forward – or possibly to the left or right. Don't worry if your pole gets stuck in the sticky riverbed; it's better to let go and paddle back – hanging from the pole and watching your punt float away is highly entertaining for an audience, but decidedly cold and wet for the "victim". Top tip: Tie your Pimm's and lemonade to the punt and hang them over the side in the water. Add some strawberries and mint for the perfect, ice-cold summer drink! Punts are available at Folly Bridge **(122 B4)** (*↷ F7*) *(Apr–Oct. | £20/ hr | www.salterssteamers.co.uk)*, Magdalen Bridge **(122 C3)** (*↷ G6*) *(Feb–Nov | £22/hr | www.oxford punting.co.uk)* and Cherwell Boathouse **(118 B5)** (*↷ F3*) *(mid Mar–mid Oct, £16/hr | www.cherwellboathouse.co.uk)*. Expect to pay a deposit of at least £50.
Exercising is more fun with others than on your own: every Saturday at 9am, people meet up for Park Run, a 5 km/ 3.1 mi race at the Cutteslow and Sunnymede Park, and afterwards head to the San Remo Café for coffee and a chat. All you have to do is register (which is free): *www.parkrun.org.uk/oxford*

FOOD & DRINK

Everyone is into cooking programmes these days – and whether you're team "Great British Bakeoff" or team "Masterchef" both shows are bound to whet your appetite.

Two celebrity chefs Marco-Pierre White and Raymond Blanc, both have extremely popular restaurants in Oxford, *Marco's New York Italian (73 High Street)* and the *Brasserie Blanc (71/72 Walton Street)*. *Fair trade* and *organic products* are very popular, and dietary restrictions such as gluten-, dairy- and nut-free, plus other allergies, are not a problem anywhere in Oxford. The pubs usually serve good, down-to-earth food, generally at reasonable prices and based on the traditional *meat and two veg* such as fish 'n' chips and *pies*, but burgers and

lasagne as well, usually served with chips and peas. On Sundays, you can't beat a good old Sunday roast. During the week, sandwiches and soups are a popular lunch option. International cuisine is everywhere, and in particular thousands of different types of curry. *Tea* (black tea with milk) is drunk at any and every time of the day and night. Tap water is widely available. If you've not tried Pimm's yet... then this delicious summer punch comes highly recommended. It is diluted with lemonade and topped with strawberries and mint, and often a slice or two of cucumber as well. Cheers!

AFTERNOON TEA

Please, please, whatever you do, don't

Cuisine for citizens of the world: from pub to gourmet restaurant, afternoon tea to exciting international dishes

go home without trying *Afternoon Tea*! Whether it's a basic version with scones, clotted cream and jam or the upgraded version, *High Tea* which also comes with cucumber, smoked salmon and/or egg sandwiches and tiny cakes on a three-tier cake stand – and often a glass of sparkling wine as well.

THE GRAND CAFÉ ★ ●
(122 C3) (ℳ G6)
Coffee culture and more! The site of Oxford's first coffee house in 1650 is now a

venue with a luxurious marble and gold-leaf interior where you can enjoy your high tea with petits fours, champagne or a cocktail. *Mon–Thu 9am–6.30pm, Fri–Sun 9am–7pm | 84 High Street | tel. 01865 204463 | www.thegrandcafe.co.uk*

THE ROSE ⓥ (122 B3) (ℳ F6)
Seasonal organic products grown locally, everything is fresh, home-made and delicious. History-lovers can find out more about the history of this small restaurant and tea room over a delicious

Don't fly over the handlebars: but it's worth braking for the Handle Bar Café

cup of tea as they read the pretty inscription along the walls. *Mon–Sat 9am–7pm, Sun 10am–6pm | 51 High Street | tel. 01865 244429 | www.the-rose.biz*

VAULTS & GARDEN CAFÉ ★ ◉
(122 B3) (⌀ F6)

In Oxford's most unusual café, you sit in the university's old assembly building of 1320, or outside amongst the gravestones of St Mary's, with an unbeatable view of the Radcliffe Camera. Too cold? *Never* – thanks to blankets and hot water bottles. The ingredients used here are all fresh, organic and local. *Daily 8.30am–6pm | Radcliffe Square, University Church | tel. 01865 279112 | www. thevaultsandgarden.com*

BLINNER

Blinner is the new brunch: breakfast, lunch and dinner! Here are some of the places where you can easily spend the whole day.

CAFÉ COCO (123 D4) (⌀ H7)

Charming atmosphere, generous cocktails, and food you just want to dive into: an iconic restaurant on the Cowley Road that serves excellent mezze, salads, pizzas, burgers and pasta. New additions to the menu: superfood porridge and gluten-free options. Yummy! *Mon–Wed 10am–10pm, Thu 10am–11pm, Fri 10am–midnight, Sat 9am–midnight, Sun 9am–10pm | 23 Cowley Road | tel. 01865 200232 | www.cafe-coco.co.uk | Moderate*

INSIDER TIP ▶ HANDLE BAR CAFÉ AND KITCHEN ◉ (122 A3) (⌀ F6)

A hidden gem: past the Bike Zone bike shop is a tiny worn staircase leading up to the first floor, then: wow! Apart from the amusing Victorian penny-farthings on the walls, there's nothing here that smacks of oily mechanics. Quite the opposite in fact: exquisite dishes made from high-quality, sustainable ingredients grown in and around Oxford will have your taste buds turning somersaults here all day long. Be sure to try the banana bread – it's heavenly! *Mon/ Tue 8am–7pm, Wed–Fri 8am–11pm, Sat 9am–11pm, Sun 10am–6pm | 28–32 St Michael Street | tel. 01865 251315 | www. handlebaroxford.co.uk | Moderate*

THE NOSEBAG (122 A3) *(㎍ F6)*

A steep staircase leads up to this iconic "feeding bag". Find your seat first, ideally in the semi-circular bay under the bottle-glass window-panes, then go to the counter to make your choice. Everything is home-made, from the crispy salads to the baked potatoes to the at least 12 different cakes that are freshly baked every day – and there's an excellent vegetarian selection, too. Also available: postcards by the Oxford artist Rosie Howlett. *Mon– Thu 9.30am–10pm, Fri/Sat 9.30am– 10.30pm, Sun 9.30am–9pm | 6–8 St Michael's Street | tel. 01865 721033 | www. nosebagoxford.co.uk | Budget*

TICK TOCK CAFÉ (123 D4) *(㎍ G7)*

Tick, tock, time is moving on – but don't worry. Within these four walls, hung with all sorts of amusing clocks, you can spend all day over your breakfast. Especially popular with students – who are sometimes still in their PJs! – for the *all-day breakfast*. Order a mug of strong tea and it will set you up for a day's sightseeing. *Daily 8am–8pm | 3–5 Cowley Road | tel. 01865 200777 | Budget*

CAFÉS

BAREFOOT OXFORD (121 F1) *(㎍ E5)*

They started out by supplying other cafés with their fabulous cakes (with tremendous success), and now Emily and Fraser have finally opened their own café in Jericho. Enjoy coffee and cake on Grandma's floral porcelain – the cakes are truly extraordinary: how about green kale and apple cake, or perhaps a beetroot muffin? Vegan options available, and everything to take away if you wish. Also sells the heavenly, luxurious creations by Oxford chocolatiers *Plantation Chocolates*. *Mon–Fri 8am–5pm, Sat/Sun 9am–5pm | 74A Walton Street | www.barefoot oxford.co.uk*

THE BEAR & THE BEAN (123 D4) *(㎍ H7)*

Super-cool merger between the *Keen Bean Coffee Club* in the Truck Store opposite, and the record, fashion and art label *Bear on a Bicycle*. Lomography cameras, ironic postcards, records and CDs, hipster T-shirts, coffee, tea and brownies.

MARCO POLO HIGHLIGHTS

★ **Cherwell Boathouse**
Fine dining in the perfect, hidden location → p. 54

★ **Edamame**
Sushi queues outside the Japanese → p. 57

★ **The Grand Café**
Tea-time amongst the marble pillars→ p. 51

★ **The King's Arms**
Pies and ales amongst the books → p. 58

★ **Thirsty Meeples**
Meeting-place for gamers → p. 54

★ **The Trout Inn**
Idyllic country pub, just like something out of a picture book → p. 59

★ **Vaults & Garden Café**
Cemetery with views → p. 52

Mon–Fri 8.30am–6.30pm, Sat 9am–6.30, Sun 10am–6pm | 98 Cowley Road | @the-bearandthebean

G&D'S

Good gelato has been available in Oxford since Stroup opened his first independent ice cream parlour! Today there are three branches of G&D in Oxford, and the ice cream is still lovingly made by hand. The combination of ice cream and bagels is unbeatable – and there's often live music at the Cowley Road branch. *Daily 8am–midnight | 55 Little Clarendon Street* (122 A2) *(ꞁ E5), 94 St Aldate's* (122 B4) *(ꞁ F6) and 104 Cowley Road* (123 D4) *(ꞁ G7) | www.gdcafe.com*

EUROPEAN

CHERWELL BOATHOUSE ⭐
(118 B5) *(ꞁ F3)*

In a picturesque location on the banks of the Cherwell: this exclusive restaurant with a tremendous selection of special wines. In summer you can sit outside on the terrace and watch the punts gliding past. Six-course *tasting menu*, live music and theatre performances. Inexpensive option: the INSIDERTIP *Teahut Bar and Café* serves small snacks and refreshments outside. Punt, canoe and rowing boat hire from mid-March until mid-October. *Mon–Fri noon–2.15pm and 6pm–9pm, Sat/Sun noon–2.30 and 6pm–9.30pm | 50 Bardwell Road | tel. 01865 552746 | www.cherwellboathouse. co.uk | Expensive*

GEE'S RESTAURANT & BAR
(118 A6) *(ꞁ E4)*

A declaration of love to Mediterranean cuisine: exclusive cuisine and wines, enjoyed amongst the climbing plants in this Victorian conservatory. The *Express Lunch* is the ideal choice for the economically-minded and for people in a hurry. *Sun–Thu 10am–10.30pm, Fri/*

FAVOURITE EATERIES

Kaboom! Superhero fast food

What would you say to a Dead Elvis Burger with Danger Fries, followed by The Baconator Milkshake? Hasta la vista, baby! At the amusing 1980s-style comic paradise *Atomic Burger* *((123 D4) (ꞁ H7) | Daily 11.30am–10.30pm | 92 Cowley Road | tel. 01865 790855 | www.atomicburger.co.uk | Budget)*, the bold can take up the Fallout Challenge: anyone who manages to eat the vast triple-decker burger in under 45 minutes receives the highly-coveted Survivor's T-shirt. Chomp, gurgle, swallow, burp, gulp, oooffff – respect!

Cafés for games

If you don't find anything that appeals amongst the thousands of games at the ⭐ ● *Thirsty Meeples ((122 A3) (ꞁ E6) Mon–Fri 11am–midnight, Sat 9am–midnight, Sun 9am–11pm | 99 Gloucester Green | tel. 01865 244247 | www.thirsty meeples.co.uk)* which range from A for Aapep to Z for Zpocalypse, then there's no helping you – but the lovely people at the café will be pleased to help you choose. For £5 per person you can play for three hours – and there's delicious coffee and cake as well as alcoholic drinks, pies and snacks. Popular iconic address – be sure to book in advance!

Sat 9.45am–11pm | Express Lunch Mon–Fri noon–6pm | 61 Banbury Road | tel. 01865 553540 | www.gees-restaurant. co.uk | Moderate–Expensive

KAZBAR (123 D4) (𝄞 H7)

Popular tapas and cocktail bar in the East End. Spanish/Moroccan-inspired food and fabulous décor with atmospheric lanterns inside and out. On Wednesday evenings, Antonio plays delightful flamenco music in the background, while on Thursdays passion is in full swing when Fran Guitarra and his band invite guests to the flamenco fiesta. *Mon–Thu 5pm–midnight, Fri 5pm–0.30am, Sat noon–0.30am, Sun noon–11pm | 25–27 Cowley Road | tel. 01865 202920 | www. kazbar.co.uk | Budget–Moderate*

PIERRE VICTOIRE (122 A2) (𝄞 E5)

Authentic French bistro: enjoy a romantic tête-à-tête by candlelight. Of course, classics such as confit de canard and bœuf bourgignon are on the menu. Good value: *Mon–Sat Prix fixe lunch* from £8.50, *Sun–Fri Pre-Theatre Dinner* (two courses, coffee) £12.50. *Mon–Sat noon–2.30pm and 6pm–11pm, Sun noon–10pm | 9 Little Clarendon Street | tel. 01865 316616 | www.pierrevictoire. co.uk | Moderate*

PIZZA EXPRESS (122 B3) (𝄞 F6)

Pizza, pasta and salads: you'll get them all here. However, the Italian in the Golden Cross Passage also has some surprises: go up the stairs, left, and left again, and you'll find yourself in the former 12th century coaching inn, where there is a whole wall covered in **INSIDER TIP** original Tudor wall paintings! *Sun–Wed 11.30am–11pm, Thu–Sat 11.30am–11.30pm | 8 Golden Cross, Cornmarket Street | tel. 01865 790442 | www.pizzaexpress. com/oxford-golden-cross | Budget*

Board instead of drinking games: Thirsty Meeples

QUOD (122 B3) (𝄞 F6)

Dons, students and artists like to meet under the paintings here in the cool former bank, for brunch, lunch, supper or just a cocktail on the terrace. Finding it difficult to choose a pizza? *No problem* – you can have half-and-half! *Daily 7am–11pm | Mon–Fri set menu noon–6pm | 92–94 High Street | tel. 01865 202505 | www.quod.co.uk | Moderate*

TURL STREET KITCHEN ✪ (122 B3) (𝄞 F6)

Café, bar and restaurant – TSK is always the right choice. This socially committed company with lots of volunteer students is involved in all sorts of Oxford

SPECIALITIES

Banbury Cake – flaky pastry, filled with mincemeat. Banbury Cake is said to be about 400 years older than the festive 'mince pie' recipe. But which is more delicious? We'll let you decide...

Fish & chips – a firm favourite: fried fish in batter with chips, delicious with salt and vinegar. Often served in pubs.

Frank Cooper's Oxford Marmalade – so special it holds a Royal warrant! A dark, thick marmalade made from Seville oranges. The original recipe (made by his wife, Sarah-Jane) dates back to 1874.

Full English (breakfast) – also called a fry-up: bacon, sausages, tomatoes and mushrooms, fried, scrambled, or poached eggs, baked beans, hash browns and toast. The best way to start the day!

G & D's ice-cream – "committed to making the best ice cream, with the highest quality creams, eggs, cane sugar and the finest natural flavours available". And they deliver! Your only decision is which flavour to choose...

New College Pudding – one of Oxfordshire's oldest puddings. This 17th century suet pudding with dried fruit is still a hangover cure for students today!

Oxford Blue Cheese – this creamy, iconic blue cheese is produced in Burford, Oxfordshire. A must-try; it was created by the owner of the Oxford Cheese Company in the mid-1990s.

Oxford Sausages – also named Oxford Skate, but no one knows why! These skinless sausages are made from a mix of pork and veal (plus lots of herbs and nutmeg) and are shaped into a C before frying. You can buy good-quality, traditionally made Oxford Sausages at the Covered Market.

Pies – from Pieminister. Ask for the legendary 'Mothership' and you'll receive the ultimate British pie feast; a pie served with mash, peas and gravy topped with crisp shallots and West Country Cheddar.

Ploughman's (lunch) – a popular pub lunch of cheese, ham, pickled vegetables, bread – and if you're lucky; an apple.

Roast/Sunday roast – pubs often serve a roast with Yorkshire pudding, vegetables, potatoes and gravy. Bonus points for pork crackling!

projects – all the profits go to those who really need them. They make sure that the products are as sustainably produced and eco-friendly as possible. Upstairs: roof terrace (summer) and ● cosy reading room with an open fire (winter). *Daily 8am–late | 16–17 Turl Street | tel. 01865 264171 | www. turl streetkitchen.co.uk | Moderate*

INTERNATIONAL

EDAMAME ⭐ (122 B2) (*∅ F6*)

Queuing is part of the deal at Peter and Mieko Galpin's trendy mini Japanese shop opposite New College. But who cares? Edamame has been an icon for almost 20 years, and it's well worth the wait. Here, the sashimi, tonkatsu and so on are freshly made, served quickly, and taste absolutely delicious. Would you mind moving up, please? And now a sake – and kanpai! *Wed 11.30am– 2.30pm, Thu–Sat 11.30am–2.30pm and 5pm–8.30pm, Sun noon–3.30pm* `INSIDERTIP` Sushi only on Thu | 15 Holy-well Street | tel. 01865 246916 (no book-ings) | www.edamame.co.uk | *Budget*

OLI'S THAI (123 E5) (*∅ H8*)

There's normally a long waiting list, but a few stools at the bar are always `INSIDERTIP` kept free for walk-ins. Easy menu with 12 different dishes a day, all in all: sen-sa-tio-nal! The aubergine curry literally explodes on the tongue. Once you're in, everything about Oli's is simply perfect – including the prices. *Thu noon–3pm, Wed–Sat noon–2pm and 5pm–10pm, small children only at lunchtime | 38 Magdalen Road | tel. 01865 790223 | www.olisthai.com | Budget*

SHANGHAI 30 (122 B4) (*∅ F7*)

Opposite Christ Church: enjoy the au-thentic Asian cuisine accompanied by Chinese music in this 15th century estab-lishment, which is decorated in the Co-lonial style. *Mon 6pm–10.30pm, Tue–Fri noon–2.30pm and 6pm–10.30pm, Sat/ Sun noon–10.30pm | 82 St Aldate's |* tel. 01865 242230 | www.shanghai30s. com | *Moderate*

Edamame: popular Japanese food

SHEZAN (122 B3) (*∅ F6*)

Well-hidden secret at the entrance to a dark alley – don't miss it! Serves the best Indian and Balti-style curries on the first floor of a 17th century house; also a large selection of vegetarian dishes. Ask for a seat by the window overlooking High Street! *Mon–Thu noon–2.30 and from 5.30pm, Fri/Sat noon–3pm and from 5.30pm | 135 High Street | tel. 01865 251600 | www. shezanoxford.co.uk | Moderate*

PUBS

THE GARDENER'S ARMS
(117 F6) (*E4*)

Not to be confused with the pub of the same name on Oxford's North Parade! Great pub in Jericho with excellent, all-vegetarian and vegan cuisine and the only beer garden in Oxford with a natural lawn. Huge selection of special beers and vegan-friendly wines. The juicy veggie burg-

THE KING'S ARMS ★ (122 B3) (*F6*)

Popular student pub with a cosy atmosphere. According to a legend, there is a resident ghost. In the "KA" you're surrounded by hundreds of donated books, many of them very old. If you take one away, you'll release an ancient curse – better not push your luck! Enjoy a tasty *pie* or burger with your beer. Particularly good: the sweet potato chips. *Daily 10.30am–midnight | 40 Holywell Street | tel. 01865 242369 | www.kings armsoxford.co.uk | Budget*

The King's Arms: cosier than any university reading room – and you're allowed to eat here

ers are well-known far beyond Oxford's boundaries. Sunday quiz from 8.30pm, steampunk sessions, DVD and video exchange. *Mon/Tue 5pm–midnight, Wed–Fri noon–2.30pm and 5pm–midnight, Sat noon–midnight, Sun noon–11pm | 39 Plantation Road | tel. 01865 559814 | www.thegarden-oxford.co.uk | Budget*

THE OLD BOOKBINDERS (121 E2) (*E5*)

"Oxford's best kept secret since 1869" is the slogan of popular "Bookies" in Jericho. Authentic pub with a friendly atmosphere, good (French-inspired) food, and an interesting selection of beers and wines. Quiz Night on Tuesdays from 9pm, open mic night Sundays from 8.30pm. *Tue–Sat noon–midnight, Sun noon–11pm*

| 17–18 Victor Street | tel. 01865 553549 | www.oldbookbinders.co.uk | *Budget–Moderate*

THE PERCH (116 C6) (*℧ C4*)

Pretty, thatched 17th century country pub, surrounded by a secluded garden, popular for weddings and other celebrations – and for its excellent Sunday lunch. Families with muddy boots and dogs are also always welcome! There is extra seating in the conservatory, and in summer INSIDER TIP well-priced small meals such as baked potatoes are available from the "Shed" in the garden. *Daily 10.30am–11pm | Binsey Lane | tel. 01865 728891 | www.the-perch.co.uk | Moderate–Expensive*

THE PUNTER (121 E4) (*℧ D7*)

Family-friendly pub with excellent food, from fish 'n' chips to international cuisine, on Osney Island. Relax over a pint on the banks of the Thames and watch the narrowboats gently chugging by. *Mon–Sat noon–midnight, Sun noon–11pm | 7 South Street | tel. 01865 248832 | www.thepunteroxford.co.uk | Budget*

THE TROUT INN ★ (116 A2) (*℧ A2*)

This lovely gastro pub has often been used as a picturesque film location. From the terrace there are idyllic ☀ views of the Isis, accompanied by peacocks in summer. The offer includes *light bites* for small appetites, classics such as *bangers & mash*, and burgers, pasta and pizza and, of course, *cream teas*. *Daily 11am–11pm | tel. 01865 510930 | 195 Godstow Road, Wolvercote | www.thetroutoxford.co.uk | Moderate*

WHITE RABBIT (122 A3) (*℧ E6*)

Tiny popular pub with a cool atmosphere down a side street off Gloucester Green. Excellent selection of tasty pizzas. All its ales come from within a 25-mile radius. If you find yourself getting bored (which is unlikely!), you are welcome to pass some time with one of the board games. *Daily noon–midnight | 21 Friars Entry | tel. 01865 241177 | www.whiterabbitoxford.co.uk | Budget*

LOW BUDGET

Elham's Lebanese Deli **(122 A2)** *(℧ E5)*: is great for falafel with Mediterranean mezze classics for lunch and snacks. *Mon–Sat 11am–6pm | 3 Little Clarendon Street | tel. 01865 557467 | www.elhamslebanesedeli.com*

The silver 1960s iconic campervan *Pizza Artisan* **(122 B4)** *(℧ F7)* serves pizza fresh from the wood-fired oven. All the usual varieties plus a few unusual ones, such as Nutella! Don't want to eat on the street? INSIDER TIP For £1.50 you can make yourself comfortable at G&D's across the road (p.54) – there's also a discount on the ice cream. *Win-win! Daily from 7pm | St Aldate's, near Christ Church | tel. 07813 111003 | www.pizzaartisan.co.uk*

First stop for picnics! Go to Taylors **(122 C3)** *(℧ G6)* with delights such as gourmet baguettes, salads, soups, fruit, plus every kind of cheese and cold meat you can imagine without the restaurant prices *Mon–Sat 7.45am–6pm, Sun 9am–5pm | 58 High Street | tel. 01865 723152 | www.taylorsoxford.co.uk*

SHOPPING

CITY WHERE TO START?
The busy **Covered Market** (122 B3) *(∅ F6)* is the place for browsing amusing Indie shops and food outlets. The High Street ("The High") offers quality and individual shops, while the brand-new **Westgate** shopping centre is ideal for shopping and entertainment, with fashion shops, cinemas and restaurants. The hip quarter of **Jericho** in the north of the city is rather more alternative, while you'll find an interesting cultural mish-mash of shops and restaurants in the east on **Cowley Road**.

The starting point for every Oxford shopping experience? The Covered Market in the centre of the city is almost 250 years old, and even die-hard non-shoppers should visit it: a tangled collection of quirky independent shops, plus market stalls, cafés, bars and delis.

The elegant High Street contains boutiques, antique shops and cafés. Mainstream shopaholics will find everything their hearts desire on Cornmarket and Queen Street, at the Clarendon and in the Westgate Centre, while bookworms should head for Broad Street. On medieval Turl Street, you'll find shops from yesteryear, while in trendy Jericho, lamp-lit Little Clarendon Street offers fashion, gift shops and delicatessens.

Photo: Hand-carved wooden kitchen accessories at Objects of Use store

Oxford's shops and boutiques are full of quirky gifts and antiques, as well as new and cutting-edge designs

The opening times are usually Mon–Sat 9.30am–7pm, Sun 11am–5pm, but of course: Indie shops make their own rules. Pretty Oxford souvenirs are often related to "Alice in Wonderland" and the INSIDER TIP "Silence please" series from the Bodleian Library, which includes a tea set, writing utensils and much more.

Museum shops often have excellent selections of tasteful items – now, will you spend longer in the museum or in the shop?!

ANTIQUES

ANTIQUES ON HIGH ★ ●
(122 C3) (*∅ G6*)

Accompanied by the classical music which is quietly piped from the speakers, you can lose yourself in this iconic and relaxing antiques paradise: jewellery, coins, books, music, crafts, fabrics, ceramics, pictures. Or perhaps you urgently need a top hat and a folklore outfit? This and much more is available here – from over 25 traders. *Mon–Sat 10am–5pm,*

Hot, hot, hot – you have been warned: chocolate varieties at Hardys Original Sweetshop

Sun 11am–5pm | 85 High Street | www. antiquesonhigh.co.uk

NORAH'S ANTIQUES (122 B3) (*Ⓜ F6*)
This relatively small shop contains mainly pretty antique and modern silver jewellery at affordable prices. Owner Norah always has her finger on the pulse: Prince William once gave his Kate a necklace with a silver "K". How romantic – and there's one here in the range! *Mon–Sat 10am–5.30pm | 15 Turl Street*

BOOKS, COMICS & MUSIC

ALBION BEATNIK (121 F2) (*Ⓜ E5*)
"So analogue it's anal" – is the slogan of this retro bookshop in Jericho. Albion stands for England, Beatnik is a reference to the cult writer Jack Kerouac:

only mega cool literature is allowed here. Books, coffee, readings, music and eco courses in Oxford's most popular Indie bookstore. *Mon–Sat 1pm–7pm, Sun 3pm–6pm (Sun term-time only) | 34 Walton Street | www.albionbeatnik. co.uk*

BLACKWELL'S ★ (122 B3) (*Ⓜ F6*)
B.H. Blackwell opened the first tiny branch of the world-famous bookshop in 1879. Since then, there has been plenty of updating and extending, and you'll probably find just about any book you want here. Upstairs: the cosy *Poet's Corner* with solid original bookshelves from the first shop and a café around the (poet's) corner. Opposite: the special *Art and Poster Shop*, next door: *Blackwell's Music. Mon, Wed–Sat 9am–6.30, Tue 9.30am–6.30pm, Sun*

11am–5pm | 48–51 Broad Street | www.
bookshop.blackwell.co.uk/bookshop

INKYFINGERS (123 D4) (*M G7*)

Indie and mainstream comics, graphic novels and Manga for all ages, including publications by the Oxford children's comic publisher "The Phoenix" *(www. thephoenixcomic.co.uk)*. Plant yourself on the sofa with a cup of coffee (roasted just around the corner at *Jericho Coffee Traders)* among kindred spirits, and lose yourself in the adventures of Batman and co. *Tue noon–7pm, Wed–Fri noon–7pm, Sat 10am–7pm, Sun 11am–5pm | 38 Cowley Road | www.inkyfingers.net*

TRUCK STORE (123 D4) (*M H7*)

Oxford's central address for *independent music:* CDs, records, record players, gig tickets and extremely good coffee from Mostro Coffee. Live music is the heart of the Truck Store – Oxford bands such as Stornoway and Glass Animals have already performed on the tiny stage, as well as others from further afield such as The Wedding Present and We are Scientists. *Mon–Fri 9.30am–6.30pm, Sat 10am–7pm, Sun 11am–6pm | 101 Cowley Road | www. truckmusicstore.co.uk*

CULINARY TREATS

FUDGE KITCHEN (122 B3) (*M F6*)

One word: wow! How can cream and sugar taste so good? It's hard to resist the generously-sized samples. And while you're engrossed in watching the sweet delights being created, without realising it another piece of fudge or toffee finds its way into your mouth... and you've bought a bag of Rocky Road. *Mon–Sat 10am–6pm, Sun 10am–5.30pm | 5 Broad Street | www. fudgekitchen.co.uk*

HARDYS ORIGINAL SWEETSHOP (122 C3) (*M G6*)

Ah, the magic of colourful sweets in a jar. Filled to the rafters with lollipops, all sorts of chocolate and retro candy from all over the world. Sugar addicts of all ages can meet here as a self-help group... or just buy a bag of lemon sherbet and leave. *Mon–Sat 9.30am–6.30pm, Sun 10.30am–6pm | 52 High Street | www. hardyssweets.co.uk*

OXFORD CHEESE COMPANY (122 B3) (*M F6*)

Exceptional delicatessen in the Covered Market. The variety *Alice*, for instance, is a sausage-shaped goat's cheese, *Oxford Isis* is made from cow's milk and the rind is washed in honey mead, and the recipe for *Oxford Sauce* (a spicy, fruity sauce that is served with pies and meat) is more strictly guarded than that of

MARCO POLO HIGHLIGHTS

⭐ **Antiques on High**
Pure heaven for collectors
→ p. 61

⭐ **Blackwell's**
For bookworms: five floors and a basement full of books
→ p. 62

⭐ **Covered Market**
Useful things, amusing things and tasty things under the same roof → p. 64

⭐ **Scriptum**
This is where Harry Potter would buy his magic wand → p. 69

⭐ **Objects of Use**
Lovely to hold: iconic everyday items → p. 69

Coca-Cola. But nothing can beat the creamy iconic blue cheese *Oxford Blue* – which also makes a great souvenir in a retro stone jar. *Mon–Sat 9am–5pm | Covered Market | www.oxfordcheese. co.uk*

THE WHISKY SHOP (122 B3) *(* *F6)*
Friendly expert advice on... yes, that's right – whisky. A huge selection of exclusive bottles, miniatures, gift sets, bar snacks and accessories for alcoholic drinks, with prices ranging from £5 to £1,000 per item. *Mon–Sat 10am–6pm, Sun noon–4pm | 7 Turl Street | www. whiskyshop.com*

LOW BUDGET

Messy paradise! You simply have to see Unicorn **(122 B3)** *(F6)*! Owner Eva has neither Internet nor telephone – she's too busy rummaging her way through the mountains of second-hand clothes and accessories. Feel free to rummage with her – there are no set prices; Eva decides on the spur of the moment how much something costs. Popular with prop-buying assistants and people with plenty of time!

A sign reminds visitors that this was the site of the very first ever Oxfam **(122 B3)** *(F6)* charity shop in 1947. A great place to find bargains: clothes, jewellery, games, coins, and videos and music in the basement. *Mon–Wed 9.30am–5.30pm, Thu 9.30am–7pm, Fri/Sat 9.30am–5.30pm, Sun 11am–4pm | 17 Broad Street | www.oxfam.org.uk*

BICESTER VILLAGE (O) *(O)*
Go on a hunt for designer fashions at bargain prices at Bicester Village, 20 km/12.4 mi north of Oxford: 130 fashion and accessory outlets with names ranging from Alexander McQueen to Vivienne Westwood offer discounts on certain items all year round. The S5 or X5 buses (from Magdalen Street) will get you there from the city centre in 30 minutes. *Mon–Sat 9am–7pm, Sun 10am–7pm (some shops open a little later on Sunday) | 50 Pingle Drive, Bicester | www. bicestervillage.com*

BOSWELL & CO. (122 A3) *(F6)*
A really nice, old-fashioned independent department store. The maze-like interior on three floors has simply everything – and is particularly well-known for toys, household goods and luggage. The pleasant, recently opened café *1738 Tearoom*, named after the year the shop opened, is the perfect place to recover from the stress of shopping. *Mon–Wed and Fri 9.30am–6pm, Thu 9.30am–6.30pm, Sat 9am–6pm, Sun 11am–5pm | 1–4 Broad Street | www. boswells.co.uk*

COVERED MARKET ★ ●
(122 B3) *(F6)*
Absolute shopping highlight with exceptional offers. Today you can find almost anything here, from half a wild boar and rare specialist cheeses to used clothing and bunches of flowers. Start by getting your bearings at Georgina's Café, then shop for some clothes at Burrows and Hare (for him) and Next to Nothing (for her), have something custom-made for your head at the Hat Box, then recover from it all over a

pie from the Pieminister. *Opening times apply to the market hall – the shops may open at different times, especially at weekends (check online): Mon–Sat 8am–5pm, Sun 10am–4pm | Market Street | www.oxford-coveredmarket.co.uk*

WESTGATE (122 A4) *(⫶ E7)*

This new shopping centre to the west is intended to reflect the origins of the working and brewing quarters in which it stands – with the use of robust materials such as wood, stone and glass. Clever bridges and escalators between the building complexes are a post-modern greeting to the twisting and turning medieval structure of the old town. The shopping centre is dominated by the flagship of the John Lewis chain. *Mon–Fri 10am–8pm, Sat 9am–8pm, Sun 11am–5pm | Castle Street | www.westgate oxford.co.uk*

MARKETS

BITTEN STREET FOOD MARKET
(122 A3) *(⫶ E6)*

If you happen to be in Oxford at the beginning of the month between March and October, visit the award-winning street food market (first Saturday of the month) in the castle quarter. Selected retailers offer everything that even the most exotically-minded foodie could desire, from locally grown courgetti (spaghetti made from spiralised courgettes) to Tibetan dumplings. *Castle Quarter | Mar–Oct, first Sat of the month, 11am–3.30pm | www.bittenoxford.co.uk/bitten-street*

GLOUCESTER GREEN MARKET
(122 A3) *(⫶ E6)*

The popular market with over 100 stalls is set up every Wednesday, Thursday and

Covered Market: shopping with atmosphere – more than a touch of history

Nothing off-the-peg: Olivia May has individual garments by innovative designers

Saturday. Fruit, vegetables and bric-a-brac are always for sale. But it's especially interesting if you come on a Thursday or Saturday, which is when you will also find stall-holders selling antiques, crafts, vintage and street food. On the first and third Thursday of the month, there is also the *Farmer's Market* with delicious, sustainably grown products from the region. *Wed/Thu 9am–4pm, Sat 10am–5pm | Gloucester Green*

FASHION, SHOES & ACCESSORIES

OLIVIA MAY (122 A2) (*⌂ E5*)
Secret tip for fashion-lovers: following her successful career as a top stylist, Ann Campbell started her trendy fashion treasure chest in popular Jericho. Experiment with one-off items by innovative designers such as Rundholz, Walla and Lilith. "Does it suit me?" – style advice is included. You will also find matching shoes, jewellery and accessories here. *Mon–Sat 10am–5.30pm | 31 Little Clarendon Street | www.oliviamay.org*

RAINBOW & SPOON BOUTIQUE (121 F3) (*⌂ E6*)
A long, narrow wooden shed is home to this entertaining shopping experience: original, but wearable and above all affordable ladies' fashion, jewellery, bags, accessories and gifts, mostly *fair trade*. Amanda Suliman-Bell runs the family business that was founded by her parents, designers June and Sam Suliman, with a personal touch. *Mon, Wed–Sat 10am–5.30 | 22 Park End Street | www.rainbowandspoon.co.uk*

SHOE EMBASSY (122 B3) (*⌂ F6*)
The "Shoe Embassy", the retail sensation from London's Brick Lane Market – now also in Oxford. The finest leather shoes, innovative designs, sexy, but oh so comfortable that you will never want to take

them off again. *Mon–Sat 10am–7pm, Sun 11am–5pm | 22 High Street | www.shoeembassy.com*

WALTERS OF OXFORD (122 B3) (*M F6*)
Unique: a traditional Gentleman's Outfitter. Academic robes, boating blazers, mortarboards and Masonry garments, but also normal suits, shirts, ties and cufflinks, to buy or hire. And to complete the exclusive overall look, buyers can pop upstairs to the barber on the top floor (see p. 79). *Mon–Sat 9am–5.30pm | 10 Turl Street | www.walters-oxford.co.uk*

SECOND-HAND & VINTAGE

THE BALLROOM EMPORIUM (122 C4) (*M G7*)
Fairy-tale ball gowns with vintage and current, pre-loved items. Wedding and other festive items, dinner jackets, long gloves, feathered masks, Art déco jewellery and much more to admire, hire and possibly buy. *Mon–Thu 10am–5.30pm, Fri 9.30am–5.30pm, Sat 9.15am–5.45pm | 5&6 The Plain | www.ballroomemporium.co.uk*

INDIGO ⊙ (123 D4) (*M H7*)
100% ethically correct organic shop – but there's no food! Clothes for him, her and baby, gifts, jewellery, accessories and homeware by eco brands such as People Tree, Komodo, Privatsachen and Made. *Mon–Fri 10am–6pm, Sat 10am–5pm, Sun 11am–5pm | 62 Cowley Road | www.shopindigo.co.uk*

SOUVENIRS & KNICK-KNACKS

ALICE'S SHOP (122 B4) (*M F7*)
An enchanting little shop with souvenirs and *sweet nothings*, and everything based on "Alice in Wonderland". Alice

SPOTLIGHT ON SPORTS

● *Bumps Races* – iconic boat race in rowing eights: the Torpids at the beginning of March and the *Summer Eights* in May. *Torpid* means lethargic, which used to be the sarcastic name for the second rowing team. Of course, no one is lethargic here, because it's about nothing less than the honour of the college: the colleges compete against each other in the Torpids and the Eights. Because the Thames, or rather the Isis, is so narrow in Oxford, the boats can't get past each other, so they have staggered starting times and then try to catch each other up and bump each other. It starts when the cannon is fired: from Iffley Lock to Folly Bridge. In the college courtyards, proudly written INSIDER TIP chalk graffiti is displayed when the college team is bumped. Successful bumpers are rewarded with the highly-coveted blades of honour. Main objective: the ultimate winning team is crowned "Head of the River" – which explains the name of the pub (p. 77) at Folly Bridge! Christ Church Meadow is a great place for watching the event, although the atmosphere is usually the most exciting a few steps further south in one of the college boathouses on Boathouse Island along the banks of the Thames. Go to *www.sport.ox.ac.uk* and "Student Sport" for a map with all the sports complexes and playing grounds.

Liddell, the little girl on whom the more famous Alice was based, lived at Christ Church across the road, and did actually shop here 200 years ago. Lewis Carroll incorporated the shop in his surreal stories. *Sun–Fri 10.30am–5pm, Sat 10am–6pm, Jul/Aug daily 9.30am–6.30pm | 83 St Aldate's | www.aliceinwonderland shop.com*

BODLEIAN SHOP (122 B3) (*ill F6*)

The library shop not only has pretty, affordable gift ideas on everything book-related, but also selected writing utensils, tableware, pictures and furniture – for instance, the iconic curator's chair will cost you £850. The best-sellers include little signs, cloth bags or towels printed with the "Bodleian Oath" – the oath that every reader has to swear before using the hallowed halls of books. *Mon–Fri 10am–5.30pm, Sat 10am–5pm, Sun 11am–5pm | Old Schools Quad and Weston Library | www.bodleianshop.co.uk*

INSIDER TIP ▶ KINA CERAMICS
(122 C3) (*ill G6*)

You can visit Karolina Gorsja in her basement studio and watch her at work creating her amusing, contemporary ceramics: The artist creates mugs with spines, cups with cheeky pin-up girls and tiny bowls shaped like speech bubbles from wafer-thin porcelain. Very special Oxford souvenir: the surreal "melting" tea set "Alice" with gold drips. At weekends, you can try your hand at making something yourself out of the clay mass (but you

Indigo: shopping with a clear conscience – and everything looks good too

must book online first). *Wed–Sun 11am–6pm | 71 High Street (through Hoyle's Games and Puzzles | www.kinaceramic design.com*

OBJECTS OF USE ★ (122 B3) (𝄞 F6)

"Against throwawayism" is the motto of this popular concept store. It's full of useful items for the kitchen and garden, for work, and for playing and relaxing. Household helpers and everyday items, attractive, high quality and long-lasting – there's no better way to combine form and function. *Mon–Sat 10am–5pm, Sun 11am–4pm | 6 Market Street | www. objectsofuse.com*

OXFORD UNIVERSITY OFFICIAL SHOP (122 B3) (𝄞 F6)

The real, genuine and only official university shop on original, medieval premises. Not only will you find the usual college hoodies, but also souvenirs such as bookstands in the shape of the Radcliffe Camera, silver spoons with the dodo and engraved crystal carafes. Just make sure there's plenty of room in your suitcase! *Mon–Sat 9am–5.30pm, Sun 11am–4pm | 106 High Street | www.oushop.com*

THE POD (122 C3) (𝄞 G6)

Soup ladle in the shape of a dinosaur, *Girly Crap* soap, pizza cutter that looks like a bicycle? Funny, hand-selected gifts – from jewellery, writing utensils, household items and party accessories, to fun items for cooking, the home and relaxing. *Mon–Sat 10am–6pm, Sun 11am–5pm | 86–87 High Street | www. thepodcom pany.co.uk*

PENS, PAPER ETC.

PENS PLUS (122 C3) (𝄞 G6)

Expert advice on everything to do with elegant writing implements. But if you're

Scriptum: stylish items for budding writers

using the new and exclusive Montblanc fountain pen, what do you write on? Well, quality handmade paper by Crane and Crown Mill, of course, or an iconic moleskin diary, which are also available here. *Mon–Sat 9am–5.30pm | 69–70 High Street | www.pensplus.co.uk*

SCRIPTUM ★ (122 B3) (𝄞 F6)

Dramatic and square: the Venetian-inspired stationery paradise has leather-bound journals, marionettes, Christmas decorations, marbles, fountain pens, bookplates, globes, model ships, miniature hot air balloons and more – much more. Bet you won't leave without buying something? *Mon–Sat 9am–5.30pm, Sun 11am–5.30pm | 3 Turl Street | www. scriptum.co.uk*

ENTERTAINMENT

CITY **WHERE TO START?**

Start your evening with a drink in the irregularly shaped iconic pub the **Turf Tavern (122 B3)** (*F6*). For a *pre-theatre meal* and a show head to the West End, although it's far more eccentric on Cowley Road in the east. Jericho is great for partying: dance the night away at a live gig or in a club.

Oxford's theatre scene is young, cheeky, experimental and always surprising. During the short reading times, student groups rehearse complex pieces with surprising professionalism.

Theatres, rock and pop, Indie and mainstream – Oxford not only has a long list of native stars, but also attracts big names from all over the world. What you shouldn't miss: in many of the college chapels, ★ ● *Evensong* is at 6pm – strictly speaking a church service, but often more like a concert *(admission free)*. A festive, centuries-old tradition, often by candle light. The choirs of New College, Magdalen and Christ Church are world-famous. Check the college websites for the exact times.

Whatever you have planned for the evening, be sure to include a visit to a pub – you'll also be able to get a decent meal at most of them.

www.dailyinfo.co.uk is your go-to website for information on current events.

Extensive theatre programme, high-quality classics, and after the performance a cosy pub or trendy club

CLUBS

ATIK (121 F3) (*[m] E6*)

Club with 5 zones: dance in the *Vinyl Decades* to retro tunes from the 70s, 80s and 90s, listen to commercial chart, house and bass at *Atik*, chill over a cocktail in the *Lounge*, juggle coconuts in the tropical interior of the *Lua Lalai*, and enjoy the people-watching in the stylish *Curve* with hip-pop, R'n'B and smooth grooves. A favourite place with friends: book a circular *booth* with table service in advance *(www.atikclub.co.uk/oxford/ booths)*! *Mon/Wed 10pm–2am, Fri/Sat 9pm–3am | From £5, Broke Mondays £1 | Park End Street | www.atikclub.co.uk/ oxford*

THE BRIDGE (121 F3) (*[m] E6*)

Super club with five zones – *The Loft:* house dance classics and bass anthems; *R&B Room:* top R'n'B and hip-hop DJs such as Charlie Sloth and Tim Westwood; *VIP Lounge:* pure classics anthems; *The Garden:* speaks for itself –

VIP tables from May to August; *Anuba:* when the place is too full, people are sent here to warm up. *Mon/Wed 10pm–2am, Thu/Sat 10.30pm–3am | You can (but don't have to) write to Billy for the guest list/VIP | 6–9 Hythe Bridge Street | tel. 07825 324372 | rsvp@bridgeoxford. co.uk | www.bridgeoxford.co.uk*

simple: every evening at 10pm (except Sundays), the burger joint changes – abracadabra – into a club, and the *cheesier* the music, the better! And instead of serving steaks and fries, the DJs at the deck now serve up good old dance classics instead. Earlier arrivals can benefit from Happy Hour (until

Beer and cocktails are the norm in Oxford – but of course, there's also wine

CELLAR (122 A3) (⌘ F6)
Hyper cool *underground location* with an amazing sound system in a tiny, narrow alley off Cornmarket Street. Live gigs plus house, electro, drum & bass, dubstep, hip-hop, reggae and ska nights. Dates on the website. *Frewin Court | www.cellaroxford.co.uk*

MAXWELL'S (122 A3) (⌘ F6)
Up the stairs to this American diner you are greeted by a glittering disco ball. Huh... ? What's that about? It's quite

10pm) before they hit the dance floor. *Mon–Sat 11.30am–11pm, Sun 11am–11pm | 36–37 Queen Street | www.facebook.com/MaxwellsOxford*

PLUSH (121 F3) (⌘ E6)
The LGBTQ club welcomes people of every sexual orientation, identity and creed. The place really rocks on Friday and Saturday evenings. Get your glad rags on, order a Fishbowl Cocktail for some group slurping, and try the pole dancing! *Welcome to the weekend! Fri/*

Sat 10pm–4am | From £4 | 27 Park End Street | Guest list/VIP (not essential): www.plushvipexperience.co.uk | www.the plushlounge.co.uk

COCKTAIL & WINE BARS

DUKE OF CAMBRIDGE
(122 A2) (*Ø E5*)

This unconventional cocktail bar in Jericho has nothing to do with the royal Prince William. And don't be put off by the reserved tables in the window – or alternatively, book one yourself *(drink@ dukebar.com)*! There's more room for chatting and chilling on the soft seats with romantically misty light chains at the back or at the bar. *Sun–Wed 2pm–midnight, Thu–Sat 4pm–1am | Happy Hour Sun–Thu 4pm–9pm, Fri/Sat 4pm–7.30pm | Cocktails from £4.95, beer/wine from £2.95 | 5–6 Little Clarendon Street | www.dukebar.com*

INSIDER TIP ▶ FREUD (121 F2) (*Ø E5*)

"Penis envy", "Death instinct" and "Phallic symbol" are not cocktails that are named after the father of psychoanalysis in this former Greek-Revival church, but the names would be appropriate! Do the large, old columns in front of the temple have a diffused blue glow? Then it's open, and you can come inside the vast open interior and enjoy cocktails, chats and dancing. More *shabby* than *chic* – "*come here to get lucky!*" There's no dress code, and students get a discount on drinks with an "F". Then perhaps a session on the couch to work through your experiences? It's up to you! *Mon–Wed noon–11pm, Thu noon–midnight, Fri/Sat noon–2am, Sun noon–10.30pm | 119 Walton Street | www.facebook.com/freudoxford*

JOE PERKS (123 D4) (*Ø H6*)

Joe Perks, cocktail pioneer and man about town, disappeared from London in the 1970s and was never seen again. Or was he...? If he were ever to pop up again, it would probably be at the ultra-cool bar named after him in East Oxford. Eclectic, comfortable ambience, walled and heated garden, the freshest ingredients for drinks and the irresistible *small plates* or brunch. *"Joe or no Joe – see you there!" Mon–Thu 5pm–midnight, Fri 4pm–1am, Sat 11am–1am, Sun 11am–11pm | Daily Happy Hour 5pm–8pm | 76 St Clements | www.joeperksandco.co.uk*

THE OXFORD WINE CAFÉ
(122 A2) (*Ø E5*)

You can be sure of a cultivated glass of wine at this elegant establishment, which is especially popular with ladies. With at least 25 open wines, 250 varieties of bottled wine, various special whiskies, spirits and wine cocktails, you're sure to find your new favourite

★ **Evensong**
Formal choir by candlelight
→ p. 70

★ **Shakespeare in the College Garden**
Theatre in the garden → p. 79

★ **Turf Tavern**
Where the night-life starts and finishes → p. 78

★ **The Varsity Club (TVC)**
Cocktails with a view → p. 74

★ **Ultimate Picture Palace**
Art deco cinema with a history
→ p. 75

MARCO POLO HIGHLIGHTS

tipple. No room at the tables? There are also comfortable seats by the windows. They also serve cheese, fish or vegetable platters. Cheers! *Mon–Thu 8.30am–11pm, Fri 8.30am–midnight, Sat 10am–midnight, Sun 10am–10pm | 32 Little Clarendon Street | www.oxford winecafe.co.uk*

RAOUL'S (121 F2) (🗺 E5)
Without exaggeration, one of the best cocktail bars in the world – if you don't believe us, check out the Sunday Times "Top 50 Bars of the World" list! The biggest selection, the freshest ingredients, the coolest DJs – Raoul's is no. 1 on every level. Friendly bouncer James makes sure that everyone behaves themselves. Why not try mixing your own cocktail? Book the entertaining *Cocktail Pervert* crash course, with or without snacks. *Sun–Tue 4pm–midnight,*

Wed–Sat 4pm–1am | 32 Walton Street | Cocktail Perverts: bartender@raoulsbar. com or tel. 01865 553732 (from £35 per person) | www.raoulsbar.com

THE VARSITY CLUB (TVC) ★ 〰
(122 B3) (🗺 F6)
Now, don't say anything for the time being, and just come with us – here in the Covered Market through the door that says "TVC". Up the stairs, straight on, left, right, empty rooms left and right – yes, that's right, just trust us and keep going – and at last – a bar! Get yourself a drink here, then keep going up, yes, really, that's right, and now, here we go, through this door – outside and… aaaaah! Don't forget to breathe! The views! Incredible! You're right up at the top, and completely surrounded by the dreaming spires. There's nowhere cooler than up here on the ● roof terrace with an ice-cold cocktail in your hand! Whether sunshine or moonlight, the views will never fail to bowl you over. Feeling chilly? Not a problem: just wrap yourself up in one of the sheepskins on the heated seats. *Sun–Thu noon–midnight, Fri/Sat noon–2am | 9a High Street (through the Covered Market) | Roof terrace until 11pm – buy your cocktail at the bar on the bottom floor and take it upstairs with you | www. tvcoxford.co.uk*

LOW BUDGET

Strap on your angel wings and fly! Heavenly cocktails at down-to-earth prices in the sexy bar at **Angels** ((122 A2) (🗺 E5) | Daily 4.30pm–1am | Little Clarendon Street | www. angelsbar.co.uk) in trendy Jericho: Heavenly Hour every evening until 9pm.

Where to go when everywhere else is closed? Easy: INSIDER TIP▶ Hi-Lo ((123 D4) (🗺 H7) | Mon–Sat 8pm–2am (often later) | 68–70 Cowley Road), Andy and Janet's "Jamaican Place" on the multicultural Cowley Road has been "in" for decades. Reggae, Caribbean food and countless varieties of rum. Peace, man!

GIGS

THE BULLINGDON (123 E4) (🗺 H7)
Popular live, independent, venue with a cocktail bar; on cool Cowley Road. Gigs, clubs, DJs, shows. *Glee Comedy (www.glee.co.uk)* on Saturday nights. *Cocktail bar Sun–Thu 4pm–midnight, Fri/Sat 4pm–2.30am | 162 Cowley Road | tel. 01865 43 49 98 | www.the-bullingdon.co.uk*

O2 ACADEMY (123 E4) (⌕ H7)

Oxford's no. 1 venue for live concerts – this is where the stars play. A low stage, lower ceiling, the room long and narrow – if you're not a giant and want to watch the goings-on, better get there early! *Box office Mon–Sat noon–5.30pm | 190 Cowley Road | tel. 01865 8135 00 | www.acad emymusicgroup.com/o2acad emyoxford*

ULTIMATE PICTURE PALACE ★ ●
(123 D4) (⌕ H7)

Art-deco iconic cinema with an even crazier story than many of the films that are shown there – should there ever be a film about it. Which there is! Stream Philip Hind's fascinating documentary: *www.picturepalace.org.uk*. All the mainstream hits, plus art-house, classics,

The cocktails are almost of secondary importance: on the roof terrace of the Varsity Club

CINEMAS

PHOENIX PICTUREHOUSE
(121 F1) (⌕ E5)

Art-house cinema in Jericho for over a hundred years! Are you ready for a healthy dose of "The Big Lebowski"? Shown here, at regular intervals. Along with foreign language, classical, mainstream and independent showings on two screens. No cinema ticket is required for the pleasant little bar upstairs – and best of all: you can take your *White Russian* into the cinema with you! *57 Walton Street | tel. 08719 025736 | www.picturehouses.com/cinema/Phoenix_Picturehouse*

epics, indies, foreign, documentaries and – shock horror: even the occasional musical. Café bar with excellent brownies and carrot cake. Tip: Wrap up warm in winter! *Cowley Road | tel. 01865 245288 | www.uppcinema.com*

CLASSICAL

Classical music is at home in Oxford. The main venues are the Sheldonian Theatre (p. 38), the Holywell Music Room, *St John the Evangelist Church (www.sje-oxford.org)* on Iffley Road, the *Jacqueline du Pré Music Building (www.jdp.st-hildas.ox.ac.uk)* at St. Hilda's College,

The Head of the River: great place to watch the college rowing races

various churches and college chapels. You can book top-quality concerts at *www.musicatoxford.com* or by phoning *01865 244806* during the academic year (October to June).

The *Holywell Music Room* is a pretty concert hall (est. 1742) with good acoustics and offers coffee and classics *(www.coffeeconcerts.com)*: there are regular concerts at 11.15am on Sunday mornings, and afterwards concert-goers head to the King's Arms (p. 58) or the Vaults & Garden Café (p. 52) for coffee, which is included in the ticket. *32 Holywell Street | Info on the Music Faculty page at www.music.ox.ac.uk*

(p. 58) ... (p. 52)

CULTURE CENTRES

NORTH WALL ARTS CENTRE
(117 F3) (⌖ E2)
Theatre, art gallery and two studios are housed in a former Victorian swimming pool on the site of St Edward's School in Summertown. Newcomers and old hands at the comedy scene, cabaret, music and other talented performers are included in the highly varied programme. *Mon–Fri 10am–4pm, Sat noon–4pm, from 5pm on days when there is a performance | South Parade | tel. 01865 319450 | www.thenorthwall.com*

OLD FIRE STATION (122 A3) (⌖ E6)
You can drink coffee, buy art, attend workshops or watch a show here. On performance days, the café becomes a bar. The charity Crisis provides further education for the homeless from the Old Fire Station, offering courses and work experience – including in the café. *Shop: Tue–Sat 11am–6pm, café: Mon–Sat 8.30am–4pm | 40 George Street | tel. 01865 263990 | www.oldfirestation.org.uk*

PUBS WITH MUSIC

THE JERICHO TAVERN (121 F1) (⌖ E5)
Iconic pub and venue for live concerts. Artists who have performed here include big names like Supergrass, Radiohead

and Ride – while today's performers are a mix of newcomers and old friends, local bands and others from further afield. Delicious food (particularly high praise for the Sunday roasts), real ales, good wines and a heated garden – be sure to pop in! *Sun–Wed noon–11pm, Thu/Fri noon–midnight, Sat 10am–midnight | 56 Walton Street | tel. 01865 311775 | www.thejerichooxford.co.uk*

WHEATSHEAF (122 B3) (*♒ F6*)

Not to be missed: an eccentric rockers' pub down a tiny lane off the High Street. No food, but plenty of atmosphere both downstairs in the pub and upstairs in the gig room. They'll have you roaring with laughter: on Mondays during term time, the *Oxford Imps* perform their improv comedy here *(8pm | £3.50 | www.oxfordimps.com). Daily 5pm–1am | 129 High Street | tel. 01865 721156 | www.facebook.com/wheatsheaf.oxford*

THE WHITE HOUSE (122 B5) (*♒ F8*)

Warm and friendly feel-good pub that often has live music. There's something new every evening – blues, folk, local bands with music to hum along to. *Mon–Sat noon–11pm, Sun noon–9pm | 38 Abingdon Road | tel. 01865 790106 | www.thewhitehouseoxford.pub*

PUBS

THE BEAR ● (122 B3) (*♒ F6*)

Duck! There's not a lot of room in this tiny pub (supposedly the oldest in Oxford) – either upright or diagonally – but it has plenty of atmosphere. Did somebody get carried away during carnival?! No – the thousands of tie ends on the walls are the result of an exchange – a tie for a beer. A roaring log fire and the best fish 'n' chips in town. On the last Friday of the month you can gaze deep into the eyes of a collection of owls, hawks, falcons and other birds of prey outside the Bear, courtesy of *Wheatley Birds of Prey (last Friday of the month 3pm–6pm | www.wheatleybirdsofprey.com). Mon–Thu 11am–11pm, Fri/Sat 11am–midnight, Sun 11.30am–10.30pm | 6 Alfred Street | Live music Wed from 9pm | tel. 01865 728164 | www.bearoxford.co.uk*

THE CHEQUERS (122 B3) (*♒ F6*)

Just so it's completely clear: you'll recognise this historic pub down a side street by the chequers board above the inscription. When, a few centuries ago, unwanted Catholic monks were discovered in a tunnel, they were promptly walled in – you can read the whole grizzly story on a golden panel outside the pub. Today it's much more civilised, with good pub food, real ales, comfortable sofas, pool and table tennis in the courtyard. *Mon–Thu 11am–11pm, Fri/Sat 11am–11.30pm, Sun 11am–10.30pm | 131 High Street | www.nicholsonspubs.co.uk*

EAGLE AND CHILD (122 A2) (*♒ F5*)

Nickname: the Bird and Baby. This is where the Inklings used to meet – which is not a self-help group for people with tattoos, in case you were wondering, but a group consisting of J.R.R. Tolkien, C.S. Lewis and fellow writers. You'll find some faded references to them in the Rabbit Room. A delightfully old-fashioned pub with lots of alcoves and corners, and good fish 'n' chips. *Mon–Sat 11am–11pm, Sun noon–11pm | 49 St Giles | www.nicholsonspubs.co.uk*

HEAD OF THE RIVER (122 B4) (*♒ F7*)

Popular pub near Folly Bridge. With lots of hanging baskets and tubs of flowers and a busy terrace right on the Isis, it's always bustling with life – not just during the Bumps Races (p. 67). Also has

Decisions, decisions... ! Huge selection of beers at the Turf Tavern

20 pretty guestrooms that were refurbished in 2017. *Mon–Fri 7am–11pm, Sat 8am–11pm, Sun 8am–10.30pm | St Aldates | tel. 01865 721600 | www.headoftheriver oxford.co.uk*

THE RUSTY BICYCLE (123 E5) *(ɯ H8)*
You can see the bicycle that is sticking out of the wall of the Rusty in Cowley from a long way off – and it's worth a visit. It has a loyal clientele of East Oxford locals and hipsters from the surrounding area. First-class food at normal prices, based around burgers, pizzas and salads. Try the home-made *Wonks* – wonderfully flavoured shots. 50% discount on Mondays on burgers, 50% discount on pizzas Tuesday to Friday lunchtimes, quiz night on Tuesday evenings from 8pm. *Mon–Tue noon–11pm, Fri noon–midnight, Sat 10am–midnight, Sun 10am–11pm | 28 Magdalen Road | www.therustybicycle.com*

TURF TAVERN ★ (122 B3) *(ɯ F6)*
Unique: follow tiny, crooked St Helen's Passage near the Bridge of Sighs, and you'll come to Oxford's best-kept secret: The Turf. A crooked, wonky pub with its roots in the Middle Ages, lots of cosy corners and a small heated courtyard. Very good food. Popular with students (not only after the exams). *Mon–Sun 11am–11pm | 4–5 Bath Place | www.turftavern-oxford.co.uk*

THE WHITE HORSE (122 B3) *(ɯ F6)*
This tiny 16th century pub with real ales and good fish 'n' chips is half hidden down Broad Street, and has often been used as a backdrop in films and TV shows. At the back, there is a particularly cosy alcove with a table. *Daily noon–11pm | 52 Broad Street | www. whitehorseoxford.co.uk*

THEATRE

The *Creation Theatre Company (www. creationtheatre.co.uk)* specialises in unusual locations such as Oxford Castle, the Bodleian Front Quad and even an old factory. The concept behind *Opera Anywhere (www.operaanywhere.com)*

is the same – "Pirates of Penzance on Punts", anyone? Of the college theatres, the most outstanding are the *Michael Pilch Studio (www.pilchstudio.com)* at Balliol, the *O'Reilly Theatre (www.oreillytheatre.co.uk)* at Keble College, and the impressive open-air amphitheatre on the roof of the *Said Business School* on Park End Street.

BURTON-TAYLOR STUDIO
(122 A3) (*∭ F6*)

Founded by Richard Burton and Elizabeth Taylor in the 1960s, the 50-seater "BT" is part of the Playhouse, and the most intimate setting for student productions during term time. At other times, children from as young as 18 months can come here for their first stage experiences. *Gloucester Street | tel. 01865 305305 | short.travel/oxf19*

NEW THEATRE (122 A3) (*∭ F6*)

Large commercial theatre with 1,800 seats. Musicals, comedy, ballet, gigs and more. *Ticket office: Mon–Sat 10am–5pm, Sun 2½ hours before the performance | George Street | tel. 08448 713020 | www.atgtickets.com/venues/new-theatre-oxford*

OXFORD PLAYHOUSE (122 A3) (*∭ F6*)

Leading professional theatre with a mostly modern British and international programme of plays, dance, music and much more. *Ticket office Mon–Sat 10am–6pm or until the performance, closed Sun or 2 hours before the performance, 1 hour before the performance in the morning | Beaumont Street | tel. 01865 305305 | www.oxfordplayhouse.com*

SHAKESPEARE IN THE COLLEGE GARDEN ★

No one should miss the *Garden Plays* in the summer: against the incomparable college backdrop, the (mostly) Shakespearean plays performed in the open-air are a fabulous experience, and especially so at *Wadham (www.oxfordshakespearecompany.co.uk)*, *Magdalen (www.facebook.com/magdalenplayersoxford)*, Worcester and New College.

TIME TO CHILL

Ooh, look at his lovely hair!

What could be cooler than having your mane trimmed at the *Oxford University Barber's*? On the first floor of the men's outfitters *Walter's* (p. 67), you'll find the *walk-in gents barber*, founded in 1869 and instantly identifiable by the red-and-white striped barber's pole. Sit yourself down with a magazine, and let master barber Jackie turn you into a typical English gentleman – well, your hair, anyway... ! *Mon–Sat 8.30am–5pm | No appointments | 10 Turl Street | short.travel/oxf4*

Hot and cold!

Tired of sightseeing? Then warm yourself up in the sauna here, then relax with a hot stone massage, followed by a chilled glass of sparkling wine with delicate petits fours. Sounds good? Lanterns will light your way down to the underground pampering rooms at the Randolph Hotel Spa... and your tired feet from all the walking will be forgotten in a flash! *Spa with massage and afternoon tea from £99 | Beaumont Street | tel. 01865 256485 | short.travel/oxf5*

WHERE TO STAY

Accommodation is not cheap in Oxford, but it's part of the experience: from the basic student room in a college to the typical B&B, to a luxury hotel – it's all available. And with every night you spend here, you'll learn more about Oxford's idiosyncracies.

Prices shoot up between July and September because that is when the parents of language and university students bring their children here, visit them, or collect them again. It's a little quieter in August, when a lot of the locals are away on holiday. Prices also vary according to the day of the week as well as the season, so it's a good idea to try a range of dates to get the best price. If you're travelling from abroad, be warned! The boundaries between B&Bs and hotels are misty, and sometimes you'll have to pay for breakfast in a B&B, so always check carefully first! *Double rooms* have a double bed, *twin rooms* two single beds, *family rooms* several beds, and an *en suite* has its own private bathroom. A buffet and *continental breakfast* are often only toast and spreads, while a *cooked breakfast* is *The Full English. Tea and coffee-making facilities* (kettle, tea and coffee) are standard in rooms. It's always cheaper to book your hotel yourself than go through an agency, and of course the *Visitor Information Centre (15 Broad Street | www.experienceoxfordshire.org)* will be pleased to help you.

There are also lots of other pretty places to stay to the west of Oxford in the

Photo: Holywell Bed and Breakfast

From basic to elegant: Oxford's accommodation can be anything from cool to cosy, romantic or unusual

picturesque Cotswolds with its gently undulating hills and typical stone houses. The *Landmark Trust (www.land marktrust.org.uk)* has unusual types of accommodation for rent with plenty of history and atmosphere.

B&BS & HOTELS: EXPENSIVE

DE VERE OXFORD THAMES
(0) (🍴 0)
This sandstone manor house on the green banks of the Thames 8 km/5 mi south of Oxford feels like one of the colleges – although with one exception: the comfort! Unlike the city hotels, there's plenty of space – enough for tennis and croquet, an indoor swimming pool, sauna, gym and spa. Relax in the comfortably refurbished 15th-century barn with a whisky by the fire. A taxi will have you in the city centre in 15 minutes. *104 rooms | Henley Road, Sandford on Thames | tel. 01865 334444 | www.phcompany.com/de-vere/oxford-thames*

LE MANOIR AUX QUAT'SAISONS
(0) (🕮 0)

French luxury in the English country-side: 20 km/12.4 mi from Oxford is star chef Raymond Blanc's ultra ro-

Lovely and fresh: Raymond Blanc in his kitchen garden at the Hotel Le Manoir

mantic hotel restaurant, which nestles cosily against the gently undulating Chilterns. Money no object? Then treat yourself to the best room in the hotel, the *Blanc de Blanc* – it will set you back almost £1,500 for the night. Let Raymond's two Michelin stars inspire you, and after enjoying your unbeatable 7-course menu, why not take part in one of the professional cookery courses, which include a tour of the fairy-tale (kitchen) garden. Bon appétit! *32 rooms | Church Road, Great Milton | tel. 01844 278881 | www.manoir.com*

THE OLD BANK ★ (122 B3) (🕮 F6)

Luxury hotel in a top location: stylishly refurbished establishment, part 14th century, part ultra-modern. Art collector Jeremy Mogford creates his eccentric hotels (which include The Old Parsonage and Gee's Restaurant) with a tremendous passion for detail and a touch of modern art. The  INSIDER TIP views from the mini balcony in room 44 are fabulous! An excellent breakfast is served at *Quod* (p. 56), another of his establishments – on the terrace in summer. As at *The Old Parsonage,* you can borrow bicycles here free of charge and tour the city. *42 rooms | 92–94 High Street | tel. 01865 799599 | www.oldbank-hotel.co.uk*

THE OLD PARSONAGE (122 A1) (🕮 E5)

The designer-styled rooms of this historic country-house in the middle of the city combine old and new. Enjoy a cocktail with your afternoon tea on the romantically lit terrace, and relax with a good book in the library. *Bertie Wright's Parsonage Grill* is well-known far beyond Oxford's boundaries for his excellent creations. *35 rooms | 1–3 Banbury Road | tel. 01865 310210 | www.oldparsonage-hotel.co.uk*

THE RANDOLPH HOTEL
(122 A3) (🕮 F6)

THE Oxford institution. Following a major fire caused by a flambéed steak, the iconic hotel reinvented itself in 2016. Tradition and quality: *certainly*, airs and stiffness: *no way!* Suggestion for the perfect way to unwind after a busy day: the famous ● Afternoon Tea in the plush Drawing Room, then a little later a gourmet meal in the *Acanthus Restaurant,* a cocktail at the cool Cartoon Bar, and then a session playing pint inspector in the Morse Bar. *151 rooms | Beaumont Street | tel. 1865 256400 | www. macdon aldhotels.co.uk*

B&BS & HOTELS: MODERATE

ARTIST RESIDENCE ★ (0) (*m* 0)

A 25-minute drive away, in the pretty picture-perfect village of South Leigh, is the thatched, recently refurbished, ultra cool and yet ultra comfortable boutique hotel run by Justin and Charlotte Salisbury. Styled all the way through with hip artworks by artists such as Andy Doig and the Connor Brothers, Pulp Fiction meets country-house style in this historic guesthouse – an unusual combination, but it works! Michelin-starred chef Leon Smith will pamper your palette in *Mr Hanbury's Dining Room. 5 rooms | Station Road, South Leigh | tel. 01993 656220 | artist residenceoxford.co.uk*

BURLINGTON HOUSE (121 F2) (*m* E1)

The 12 stylish, minimalist rooms, all with a power shower, are in the main building and in the Zen-like, relaxed, walled Japanese garden. Host Nes is famous for his first-class breakfast with home-made yoghurt and a selection of mueslis. A ten-minute bus ride from the city. *12 rooms | 374 Banbury Road | tel. 01865 513513 | www.burlington-hotel-oxford.co.uk*

COTSWOLD LODGE (118 A6) (*m* E4)

An elegant corner building on Banbury Road. The best (and most expensive) rooms are in the Victorian manor house, the more affordable ones in the modern extension around a terraced courtyard.

Much-frequented restaurant, and the cosy lounge is popular for afternoon tea. With parking. *49 rooms | 66a Banbury Road | tel. 01865 512121 | www.cotswold lodgehotel.co.uk*

HAWKWELL HOUSE HOTEL (0) (*m* 0)

You'll find this impressive villa in the middle of an elegant park in the pleasant village of Iffley, south of Oxford. Tasteful feel-good ambience. A pleasant half-hour walk along the Thames to the city, or else it's a short bus ride away. *77 rooms | Church Way, Iffley Village | tel. 01865 749988 | www.hawk wellhouse.co.uk*

HOLYWELL BED AND BREAKFAST (122 B2) (*m* F6)

Charming B&B in a central location. Carrie and Stuart Holloway are literally bursting with hospitality and Oxford enthusiasm! Stuart is an experienced

---

MARCO POLO HIGHLIGHTS

★ **Bath Place**
As crooked as they are quaint: charming cottages in the old town → p. 85

★ **Malmaison**
Spend your holiday night in a former prison cell → p. 84

★ **Tower House**
Typically Oxford AND socially fair → p. 85

★ **The Old Bank**
Account overdrawn? Worth it for this "bank" → p. 82

★ **Artist Residence**
Eccentric country pub with artistic flair → p. 83

---

guide, and will give you a discount on one of his guided tours of the city (www.oxfordwalkingtours.com). Parking. *2 rooms | 14 Holywell Street | tel. 018 65 721880 | www.holywellbedandbreak fast.com*

REMONT OXFORD (117 E1) (*m E1*)

This makes the short bus ride to north Oxford more than worth it! The boutique hotel scores points for the abundant comfort and trendy retro design – *quality all-round*. For ultimate comfort book one of the five Superior Rooms. An easy walk to the restaurants in Summer-

town. *25 rooms | 367 Banbury Road | tel. 01865 311020 | www.remont-oxford.co.uk*

ROYAL OXFORD (121 F3) (*m E6*)

This sturdy, mustard-yellow three-star hotel in a practical location close to the station cannot be missed. Ask the lovely staff for one of the four corner rooms – they're much bigger than the others but cost the same! Breakfast is at the *Jam Factory (www.thejamfac toryoxford.com)* across the road – not always included, so check the terms of your booking. You can park at Staples for £5/day. *26 rooms | Park End Street |*

MORE THAN A GOOD NIGHT'S SLEEP

Rendezvous in a green field

Psst, listen... Ah, the silence... no noise apart from the birds and the hum of the delightful countryside! This romantic, isolated former shepherd's hut *((0) (m 0) Chipping Warden/near Banbury | tel. 01295 660066 | www.shep herdhutholidays.co.uk | Budget)* is perfect for relaxing from the city stress without being disturbed, and also without having to miss out on your home comforts (it has a lovely double bed, bathroom and mini kitchen). Relaxation and quality time à deux guaranteed! Real ponies are just as welcome as Shanks's! It's not far to *The Griffin* pub.

50 Shades of Oxford

Have you been naughty? Then there's only one thing for it: Go to your room! Ideally in a medieval castle... or even better, in an old gaol in a medieval castle... with thick walls, iron doors and barred windows... ⭐ *Malmaison*! *((122 A3) (m E6) | 95 rooms and suites |*

3 New Road | tel. 01865 689944 | www.malmaison.com/locations/oxford | Expensive). It's no good calling for help – the ancient castle walls of the rooms in 'A' Wing of the city's trendiest hotel are sound-proof but surrounded by mega cool design: the sparkle of the freestanding baths, rain showers and espresso machines competes with the *mood lighting*. Want to go a step further? Book the "Double Cell" in the House of Correction. Ooh lala!

Student accommodation for rent

At *University Rooms* you can book basic but unforgettable INSIDER TIP overnight accommodation in a college *(Budget | mostly only outside the academic year)*. Balliol, Merton, Brasenose and Magdalen are particularly popular, with cooked breakfasts in the medieval dining hall, but so is pretty little St Edmund Hall, where the porters are especially friendly. www.university-rooms.com

Bath Place has been host to Flemish weavers and students in its past; today, it welcomes tourists

tel. 01865 248432 | www.royaloxford hotel.co.uk

TOWER HOUSE ★
(122 B3) (*∅ F6*)
Individual and original rooms in this historic building opposite Jesus College – including the 13th century city walls – oh, and duck! Low ceilings, crooked staircases, narrow corridors – and bags of atmosphere. Belongs to the Turl Street Kitchen (p. 56) around the corner, which is where you go for breakfast: student commitment means that all the profits go to a charity in Oxford. *8 rooms | 15 Ship Street | tel. 01865 246828 | www. towerhouseoxford.co.uk*

B&BS & HOTELS: BUDGET

BATH PLACE ★ (122 B3) (*∅ F6*)
Cluster of charming 17th century cottages surrounding a tiny flagstone courtyard,

close to the Turf Tavern, with an illustrious history and famous fans – a brochure is available at reception. Elizabeth Taylor and Richard Burton were particularly fond of the four-poster bed in room no. 3. Parking at Merton College. *15 rooms | 4–5 Bath Place, Holywell Street | tel. 01865 791812 | www.bathplace.co.uk*

BROWNS GUESTHOUSE
(123 E6) (*∅ H8*)
You'll instantly feel like part of the family in Mary and George's cosy B&B. Daughter Jessica manages the *Café Silvie* in the same building – the food is guaranteed organic and sustainably produced. Jessica has gathered an entertaining group of artists who organise live events and their artwork, which is for sale, is displayed on the walls. INSIDER TIP Kazem Hakimi's award-winning photography is available here and at Kazem's *Chippy (fish and chips*

85

shop) next door. *11 rooms | 281 Iffley Road | tel. 07711 897168 | www.browns oxford.com*

walk from Christ Church. Check-in and breakfast are at the recently refurbished *Caffé Ethos* across the road – which also serves afternoon tea (of course!)

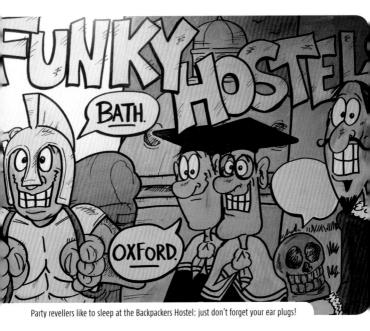

Party revellers like to sleep at the Backpackers Hostel: just don't forget your ear plugs!

THE BUTTERY (122 B3) (*ⓜ F6*)
A steep staircase leads up to the only hotel on Broad Street – you couldn't be more central! Good standards and modern interiors. Ask for rooms with views of Balliol and Trinity College. A *buttery* is a room in a college that stocks provisions for sale to students – and here it's the name of the public café serving breakfast on the ground floor (continental included, cooked costs extra). *16 rooms | 11–12 Broad Street | tel. 01865 811950 | www.thebutteryhotel.co.uk*

ETHOS (122 A5) (*ⓜ F7*)
Boutique hotel with underfloor heating, in a quiet residential area a ten-minute

and pizza. Book your parking in advance. *12 rooms | 59 Western Road | tel. 01865 245800 | www.ethoshotels.co.uk*

ISIS GUEST HOUSE (123 D4) (*ⓜ G7*)
Friendly accommodation that is available between July and September! The rest of the year, the B&B is exclusive student accommodation for St Edmund Hall. Book as far in advance as you can. *37 rooms | 45–53 Iffley Road | tel. 01865 613700 | www.isisguesthouse.com*

OLD BLACK HORSE (123 D4) (*ⓜ G7*)
Reasonably-priced accommodation in an old coaching inn above a pub. Sadly you can only park your car in the stables;

you'll have to make alternative arrangements for your horse. *9 rooms, 3 apartments | 102 St Clement's Street | tel. 01865 244691 | www.oldblackhorse.com*

RED MULLIONS GUEST HOUSE
(0) (*M O*)

Cosy B&B in the suburb of Headington with spotlessly clean, generously-proportioned, modern rooms, good breakfasts and practical bus connections to the city centre. *13 rooms | 23 London Road | tel. 01865 742741 | www.redmullions.co.uk*

HOSTELS, APARTMENTS & CAMPING

OXFORD APARTMENT
(121 E1–2) (*M D5*)

Eight stylish apartments for two to four people in a new building on the canal in Jericho, one is close to the castle. From £175 per day, with parking and internet. *tel. 01865 304024 | www.oxfordapartment.co.uk*

OXFORD BACKPACKERS HOSTEL
(121 E3) (*M E6*)

The Funky Hostel – you'll only find that here! Well, all right – and in Bath. Young, friendly, cheerful atmosphere, with a bar *(Wed–Sat)*, giant TV and kitchen. Four to 18 beds per room, also *female only*, from £16.50 including continental breakfast and bed linen. Two minutes from the station, five from the bus station. You can leave your luggage for a small fee. *9a Hythe Bridge Street | tel. 01865 721761 | www.hostels.co.uk/ Oxford-Accommodation.html*

OXFORD CAMPING AND CARAVANNING CLUB (0) (*M O*)

At the Go Outdoors superstore, you'll find a campsite that is open all year round. With planes, trains and cars around you it's not exactly quiet, but it's a cheap place to spend the night and only just over 2 km/1.2 mi to the city. Walk, run, cycle or take the bus into town. *85 pitches | 426 Abingdon Road | tel. 01865 244088 | www.campingandcaravanningclub.co.uk*

OXFORD CITY APARTMENTS

The three well-equipped apartments are located in the west of the city, one on Magdalen Road. From £530/week. *tel. 01865 300884 | www.oxfordcity apartments.co.uk*

LOW BUDGET

The Westgate Hotel (121 E3) (*M D6*) is a friendly, budget hotel near the railway station. Small breakfast garden for the warmer weather. Practical: there's a corner shop for all those bits and pieces you need when travelling (or perhaps don't need). *20 rooms | 1 Botley Road | tel. 01865 726721 | www.westgate hoteloxford.co.uk*

Not just a dormitory – the **Youth Hostel (121 E3) (*M D6*)** at the railway station also provides very private accommodation with its own bathroom. Pleasant staff, an international atmosphere and good standards at reasonable prices. Garden, café/bar. Some rooms have a balcony. Bed linen included, and towels are available for a small charge. You can park at the Seacourt Park & Ride. *47 rooms | 2a Botley Road | tel. 03453 719131 | www.yha. org.uk/hostel/oxford*

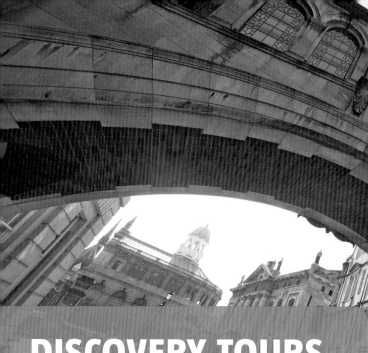

DISCOVERY TOURS

1 OXFORD AT A GLANCE

START: ❶ Vaults & Garden Café **END:** ⑱ Wheatsheaf	**1 day** walking time (without stops) **1 hour**

Distance:
 3 km/1.9 mi

 COSTS: Climbing the ❷ tower of the University Church of St Mary's £4, admission ❻ Christ Church £7, Picture Gallery £4, food and drink approx. £50

 IMPORTANT TIPS: The times apply from Mon to Sat (different opening times on Sun). If you want to do the tour on a Sunday, then start two hours later. You'll have to miss out on the Full English, but everything will balance out again with the remainder of the visits (i.e. 11.30 start – on Sundays St Mary's Tower opens at 11.30am, Christ Church 2pm).
   Book the mini tour of the ⑮ Bodleian Library in advance!

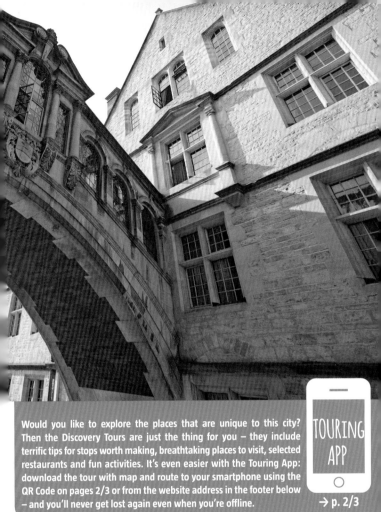

Would you like to explore the places that are unique to this city? Then the Discovery Tours are just the thing for you – they include terrific tips for stops worth making, breathtaking places to visit, selected restaurants and fun activities. It's even easier with the Touring App: download the tour with map and route to your smartphone using the QR Code on pages 2/3 or from the website address in the footer below – and you'll never get lost again even when you're offline.

TOURING APP

→ p. 2/3

Come with us on a voyage of exploration! Let us show you Oxford's must-see highlights and secrets that only a few people know. Starting with fabulous views of the city's spires, Harry Potter's Christ Church, with afternoon tea and a game of pool in a 500-year-old pub followed by a curry – and finishing with some rocking out to live music. Cover all of the top sights in one sweeping blow!

09:30am Make yourself comfortable amongst the gravestones (!) and experience a Full English Breakfast (until 11.30am) at the ❶ **Vaults & Garden Café** → p. 52.

❶ Vaults & Garden Café

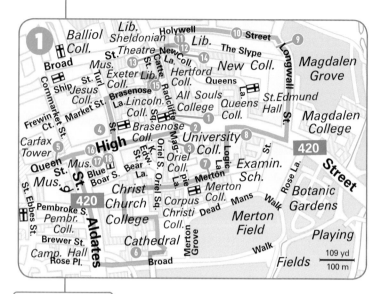

② Tower of the University Church of St Mary's 🏛 🌿

③ Oriel College 🅰

④ Covered Market 🏛 🛍

⑤ Memorial plaque to the Swyndlestock Tavern 🅰

Then the first adventure: climb the tower at the **② University Church of St Mary's → p. 34** with breathtaking views of Oxford! On the façade of **③ Oriel College** *(Oriel Square | www.oriel.ox.ac.uk)* opposite: high up on the wall, between two pillars, is an unassuming INSIDER TIP gentleman made of stone, dressed in a suit and with his hat in his hand. Generous sponsor of the academic elite – or imperialist racketeer? Opinions are divided regarding Rhodes, the founder of Rhodesia (today Zimbabwe) and the Rhodes sponsorship. Following student protests under the hashtag #RhodesmustFall, Oriel College considered its options, and finally made the decision: *"Like it or not"* – Rhodes stays. Blue-and-white flags indicate the entrances to the **④ Covered Market → p. 64** – explore Oxford's historic shopping centre, with its many little alleys and irresistible indie shops. **Then continue straight on to the Carfax Tower → p. 43**, and opposite the Santander bank you'll see the **⑤ memorial plaque to the Swyndlestock Tavern → p. 14. Turn left onto St Aldates, past the town hall and Tom Tower, then go left again and through the large gate** with the pretty War Memorial Gardens to your left and Christ Church Meadow to your right → p. 31.

11:30am The entrance to ⑥ **Christ Church → p. 29** is **on the left side of Broad Walk**. You'll find the backdrops to the Harry Potter films, fabulous buildings and court-yards, and the **cathedral**. Art lovers will be delighted by the masterpieces in the exquisite **Picture Gallery → p. 30**. **From Christ Church you'll come to Merton Street**, where on the left and a little set back is the tiny shop of the ⑦ **Oxford University Tennis Club → p. 24**. If you're in luck, the tennis court will be in use and you'll have a chance to watch this rather unusual ball game! **Then follow Logic Lane to High Street, where you'll turn right.**

02:00pm It's time for a *late lunch*, ideally at the ⑧ **Grand Café → p. 51 on High Street**: How about a Grand High Tea, which includes a glass of Champagne – *why not?* Fed and watered, **cross High Street and turn left down Longwall Street** – you'll soon see why it's called that! **Just before you get to Holywell Street you'll pass some green garage doors on your left**: the ⑨ **garages of Morris Motors → p. 46** from 1905, where the future motor manufacturer started out. **Continue down** pretty ⑩ **Holywell Street** with its pastel-painted terraced

⑥ Christ Church

⑦ Oxford University Tennis Club

⑧ Grand Café

⑨ Garages of Morris Motors

⑩ Holywell Street

Prettily coloured homes on Holywell Street

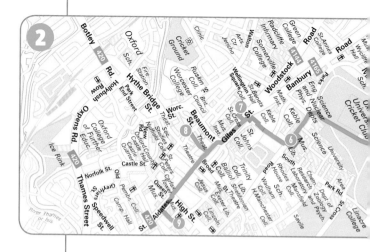

⑪ Cottages	🏛
⑫ Turf Tavern	🏛
⑬ Bridge of Sighs	🏛
⑭ Edmond Halley House	🅰
⑮ Bodleian Library	🏛
⑯ Shezan	🍴
⑰ The Chequers	
⑱ Wheatsheaf	🎵

houses: pure Oxford! In the 1950s, no. 99 was home to J. R.R.Tolkien. Leave New College behind you on the left. Now, watch out! **Turn left down narrow Bath Place**, and you'll find yourself outside a pretty courtyard with charming ⑪ **cottages** from the 17th century. **Turn left, and go through** ⑫ **Turf Tavern** → p. 78 – this twisty-turny course gets you back to New College Lane. Have a look at the ⑬ **Bridge of Sighs** → p. 36 and **side step to the left**, where you'll see a white building, the ⑭ **Edmond Halley House** *(7 New College Lane)*, with a memorial plaque to the former resident and discoverer of the comet. Now it's on to the ⑮ **Bodleian Library** → p. 34, where a mini tour will take you through the **Divinity School** → p. 35 and the medieval **Duke Humfrey's Library** → p. 36. **Follow medieval Brasenose Lane and Turl Street back to High Street,** and head for the Indian curry house ⑯ **Shezan** → p. 57 for a delicious and typical evening meal.

07:00pm Now what would you like to do – sink into a deep sofa or go for some more exercise? ⑰ **The Chequers** → p. 77 has plenty of comfortable furniture to relax in, as well as **INSIDER TIP** table tennis and pool – so you can have both. And when you've recovered, you can treat yourself to a rock gig (from 8pm) at the ⑱ **Wheatsheaf** → p. 77. *Enjoy!*

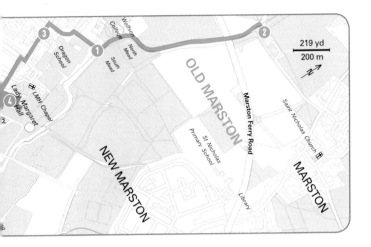

  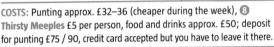

PUNTS AND PINTS

START: **①** Cherwell Boathouse END: **⑨** The Bear Inn	1/2 day walking time (without stops) 1½ hours
Distance: 🚍 4.5 km/2.8 mi	

COSTS: Punting approx. £32–36 (cheaper during the week), **⑧** Thirsty Meeples £5 per person, food and drinks approx. £50; deposit for punting £75 / 90, credit card accepted but you have to leave it there.

IMPORTANT TIPS: ① Cherwell Boathouse: Punt hire only from Mar–Oct; **⑦ Thirsty Meeples:** booking essential! **⑧ The Bear Inn:** If you want to sit down to eat, you must book in advance. **① Cherwell Boathouse:** The no. 2 bus will get you to the starting point here.

On this tour, you'll experience the most typical and most enjoyable activity that Oxford has to offer: punting. And while you're out, you'll be able to sample delicious, hearty meals in typical pubs along the way and perhaps sample a pint or two. You can then enjoy some more fun and games – literally – at the iconic gaming café Thirsty Meeples, and finish this particular experience with a delicious helping of fish 'n' chips.

12:30pm Hurray – we're heading for the water! Hire a punt from **① Cherwell Boathouse** → p. 54: not so many tourists come here, yet the Cherwell is wider and calmer,

① Cherwell Boathouse

and you can INSIDER**TIP** take your time to understand how to boat Oxford style. The lovely staff at the Boat-house will be pleased to help you and show you a few tricks. Punt (about half an hour upriver) to the **②** **Victoria Arms** *(Mon–Fri 11.30am–3pm, 5.30pm–11pm, Sat 11.30am–11pm, Sun noon–11.30pm | Mill Lane | tel. 01865 241382 | www.victoriaarms.co.uk | Moderate)* in Old Marston. Enjoy a well-earned lunch after your endeav-ours, ideally with a light IPA (Indian Pale Ale). How about *ox cheeks with black pudding*? Back to the Boathouse now – and it'll be a little easier, as the going's downriver.

② Victoria Arms 🍽

04:00pm Now enjoy a pleasant stroll **down Dragon Lane towards Norham Gardens back to the city**. On the way you'll see the **③** **Dragon School** *(Bardwell Road | www. dragonschool.org)*: which tames young children rather than dragons. Several famous actors have been educat-ed here, including Emma Watson, Hugh Laurie and Tom Hiddleston. **Dragon Lane gets narrower and narrower until it goes right onto Norham and then immediately left onto Fyfield Road. Turn left into Norham Gardens.** A secret tip from us: the INSIDER**TIP** **enchanting garden** at **④** **Lady Margaret Hall** *(daily 10am–5pm | Admission*

③ Dragon School 🏛

④ Lady Margaret Hall 🌳

You've earned it: relax at the Victoria Arms after punting

free | Norham Gardens | www.lmh.ox.ac.uk). "LMH" was founded in 1878 as Oxford's first college for women. Go past the tennis courts down to the Cherwell; it's a delightful, peaceful part of the area. **Stroll on through ⑤ University Parks → p. 41. Go through the gate on Parks Road and continue south**. You'll soon pass the ⑥ **University Museum of Natural History → p. 40** – look out for the **dinosaur footprints** on the grass outside and the **Darwin Evolution Column** outside the elaborate entrance! **Follow Museum Road to wide St Giles** with the famous ⑦ **Eagle and Child → p. 77** pub on the opposite side.

`05:00pm` Continue along St Giles to the city centre. **Turn right down the narrow passage called Friars Entry towards the Gloucester Green market place.** Now you can have a rest and a pie at the entertaining gaming café ⑧ **Thirsty Meeples → p. 54**. It's the perfect place for a friendly session of board games. Which, as we all know, really gives you an appetite, so **continue along Cornmarket Street to Blue Boar Street, and turn left at the Alfred Street corner** to the tiniest pub in Oxford: ⑨ **The Bear Inn → p. 77**. Treat yourself to a portion of fish and chips with *salt and vinegar*. And a local beer: Shotover Scholar. Delicious! If you find it's starting to get fuller and more cramped, there's a reason for this: it's Wednesday, and there's live music from 9pm!

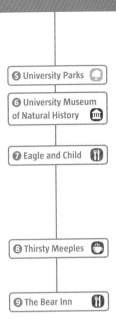

⑤ University Parks

⑥ University Museum of Natural History

⑦ Eagle and Child

⑧ Thirsty Meeples

⑨ The Bear Inn

---

③ COUNTRY OUTING: CASTLE, MEADOW, HOLY FOUNTAIN

START: ① Oxford Castle END: ⑧ Home Close	1 day walking time (without stops) 2 hours
Distance: 🚶 7.7 km/4.8 mi	

COSTS: About £11 for the tour of ① **Oxford Castle**, £2.10 bus, food and drinks approx. £50
WHAT TO PACK: Sturdy shoes for ③ **Port Meadow**. It can get muddy when it rains.

IMPORTANT TIPS: Book the tour of ① **Oxford Castle** in advance. The no. 6 bus departs from the stop at ⑧ **Home Close** *(Mon–Sat every 15 mins, Sun every 30 mins, last bus at 11.20pm | £2.10)* back to the city.

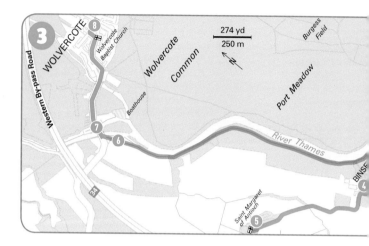

On this tour you'll get to know all about Oxford Castle, the oldest building in the city, from top to bottom. After that, some picturesque natural sights await you: unspoilt, medieval countryside is hidden between Oxford's waterways, a natural landscape with cows, horses and rare wild flowers. Discover the secret of Binsey, the ancient place of pilgrimage, then stroll past the bat-inhabited ruins of a former convent, and enjoy the rests in two idyllic pubs.

❶ Oxford Castle 🏰 🍽

10:00am The day begins with "Oxford Castle Unlocked", a tour with costumed guides of ❶ Oxford Castle → p. 44 including St George's Tower and the medieval crypt. Rebellious students were already being locked up here in the Middle Ages. Order a cup of coffee at the Castle Yard Café (daily 10am–5pm | oxfordcastlequarter.com/attractions/castle-yard-cafe | Budget)

12:00pm Follow Tidmarsh Lane, at the end take a quick left, then turn right onto pretty Fisher Row, which follows the river. After a few metres walk up to the bridge at the Oxford Retreat pub, cross Hythe Bridge

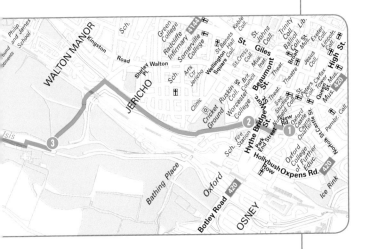

Street, and then take the path down to the canal.
Follow this picturesque ❷ **path** between the two waterways of the Castle Mill Stream and the Oxford Canal, which was built by prisoners in the 18th century.
In bygone days, coal used to be brought from Coventry
in the Midlands to Oxford and then down the Thames
to London; today, the houseboats gently bob about.

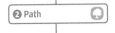

❷ Path

You no longer see working boats here: the Oxford Canal follows the countryside

3 Port Meadow 	Cross an iron bridge, go up a ramp on the left at the next bridge, then turn left onto Walton Well Road. After about 100 m/328 ft you'll find yourself at the end of the road, and you'll get your first impression of the vast expanse of **3 Port Meadow** → p. 46. **Ignore the gate on the right, and go through the double gate onto the meadow. Now follow the footpath across the meadow to the trees (about 300 m/984 ft away).** You'll soon see a bridge with a little gate. **Follow the bridge over the Isis onto narrow Fiddler's Island, and at the end cross the red iron Rainbow Bridge.** You'll soon see the thatched pub **4 The Perch** → p. 59 **in tiny Binsey.**

4 The Perch

01:00pm Stop here for some lunch to recharge your batteries: in cold weather, settle down beside the roaring open fire – and if you come in summer, get a snack from the *shed* in the garden. Take a little detour on the way back: **go past the pretty little cottages and enjoy the stroll through the countryside**, and you'll come to an old churchyard and the church of **5 St Margaret of Antioch** → p. 47. Discover **Frideswide's holy fountain,**

5 St Margaret of Antioch

The spirit of fair Rosamund, who is buried at Godstow Abbey, is said to roam outside the ruins

and inside the church the surprisingly shapely INSIDER TIP carving of St Margaret in the pulpit.

03:00pm Back at the pub, go through the beer garden along a lovely path down to the river. Follow the Isis north to the lock at Godstow. You'll soon see the bat-infested ⑥ **ruins of Godstow Nunnery**, since 1175 the resting-place of the "fair Rosamund", the long-term mistress of King Henry II who was allegedly lured into a trap by Queen Elinor and murdered. **Past the ruin, take the right-hand fork up to the bridge across the road, then turn right. The path crosses two more bridges.** Stop briefly at the second bridge and admire the lovely view of the Isis and your next stop: the picturesque pub ⑦ **The Trout → p. 59**, where legend has it that the spirit of the fair Rosamund is still present!

04:30pm After a delicious cream tea, **follow Godstow Road to the right, then turn right at the White Hart Inn. At the next left turn,** you'll see the bus stop ⑧ **Home Close**, where you can get the no. 6 bus back to the city centre.

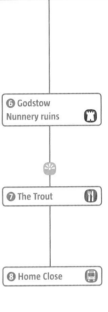

⑥ Godstow
Nunnery ruins

⑦ The Trout

⑧ Home Close

COLLEGE GARGOYLE COCKTAIL

START: ① Magdalen College END: ⑧ Raoul's	1/2 Day walking time (without stops) 1½ hours
Distance: 🚶 5 km/3.1 mi	

COSTS: Admission **Magdalen College** £5, **New College** £4, mixing cocktails at ⑧ **Raoul's** about £50, food and drinks about £50
WHAT TO PACK: Binoculars

IMPORTANT TIPS: Booking in advance is essential: Cocktail Perverts lesson at ⑧ **Raoul's** (tel. 01865 553732 | bartender@raoulsbar.com); start Fri/Sat 5pm latest, Thu–Sun 7pm
① **Magdalen College:** open Jul–Sep at noon, Oct–Jun at 1pm. From Easter until autumn, the entrance to / exit from ⑥ **New College** is on New College Lane, otherwise on Holywell Street.

Come on a tour of two very special colleges that are simply covered in gargoyles! You'll walk through the city's spookiest alleys, enjoy a cool drink with fabulous views at airy heights, and then – under professional guidance – mix your own cocktail. Cheers!

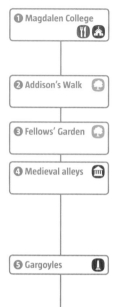

1 Magdalen College 🍴 🏠

2 Addison's Walk 💬

3 Fellows' Garden 💬

4 Medieval alleys 🏛

5 Gargoyles ❗

`12:00pm` Start the tour with a relaxed lunch right beside the Cherwell at the `INSIDER TIP` **Old Kitchen Bar** in delightful **1** **Magdalen College** → p. 32. You'll encounter some strange gargoyles, and hidden, sometimes cheeky, *misericordia* in the chapel. **Then stroll along idyllic** **2** **Addison's Walk** → p. 32 past the deer park, and if you're really lucky in spring you'll see a veritable sea of rare purple and white snake's head fritillaries in the Water Meadow → p. 32. A detour over a wooden bridge will take you on a round tour of the delightful **3** **Fellows' Garden**. **Back on High Street, turn right, then right again onto narrow Queen's Lane.** Go back in time: hardly anything has changed on these **4** **medieval alleys** over the centuries. Particularly effective when it starts to get dark thanks to the dim light of the retro gas street lights. During the Civil War, soldiers rode their horses around here – and it is said that they still do so today… in spirit form! Now: gargoyle alarm! Just **past the first hard left** at the top of the New College wall you'll see a collection of **5** **gargoyles** → p. 21 with more or less obvious indentations on their stony faces that one would otherwise only find in a more… personal area. Use your binoculars at your own risk!

MAYDAY, MAYDAY

1 May has become something of a cult in Oxford: every year, for more than 500 years, the choristers of Magdalen College climb the Great Tower at 6am, sing a hymn from there, and then the bells chime. Why? Don't ask – this is Oxford; there doesn't need to be a reason. The night before is an all-night party – with music, food and drink, and a happy atmosphere. If you want to hear the choir, though, you'll have to be at Magdalen Bridge by 5am at the latest. And whatever you do, don't even think about jumping down into the Cherwell – firstly the water isn't very deep, and secondly it's full of revolting and, more importantly, dangerous stuff. For years the bridge was closed on 1 May because obstinate people always insisted on jumping into the shallow stream despite the horrific rate of injuries and even deaths. Jingle, tinkle, jingle, tinkle: after the hymns, the Morris Dancers lead a procession of people to Radcliffe Square, where they start performing the traditional Morris dance to the accompaniment of an accordion – and from there they move on through the city. The basic equipment for Morris dancers: bells, sticks, straw hats, coloured handkerchiefs and traditional clothes. It's mad – but everyone should enjoy this "very Oxford" experience at least once in their lifetime.

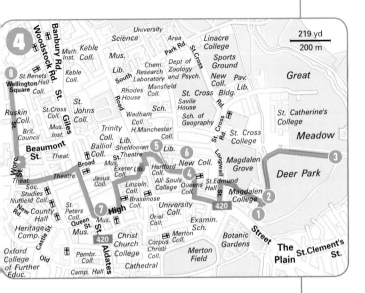

03:00pm Depending on the season, enter the legendary ⑥ **New College** → p. 37 either here (in summer), or via Holywell Street (in winter). Demonic *gargoyles*, unicorns, a movie star tree and an allegedly squeaky hill – all pretty out of the ordinary, we'd say! **After the tour, the route will take you to the end of New College Lane, then via Catte Street, Brasenose Lane and Turl Street (look up – *gargoyles*!) right onto High Street.** Don't miss the entrance to ⑦ **The Varsity Club** → p. 74 for the first cocktail of the day – with fabulous views of all the sights!

05:00pm At Carfax, turn right and follow Cornmarket and George Street to Gloucester Green. On the other side of the square go under the small underpass to Worcester Street, turn right, and then continue straight on to Jericho. You have booked a crash course in mixology at popular ⑧ **Raoul's** → p. 74 bar. Compose your own unforgettable Oxford cocktail here under expert guidance, and wind down at the end of the day in the hip quarter of Jericho.

⑥ New College

⑦ The Varsity Club

⑧ Raoul's

TRAVEL WITH KIDS

Oxford is generally geared up for students, while attractions aimed at young children are often outside the city. Within the city, the museums have fabulous events for children *(www.museums.ox.ac.uk/content/family-friendly-events.)* Backpacks full of fun materials, trails and crafts, and much more are available at the *Museum of Natural History* on Sundays from 2pm–4pm, at the *Pitt Rivers Museum* on Saturdays from 10am–4pm, and at the *Ashmolean Museum* on Sat/Sun from 10am–4pm. The *Ashmolean* and the *Museum of the History of Science* have booklets with family tours, and the *Botanic Garden* also provides materials for budding explorers. An attractive little book (and very helpful for mini travellers!) is the Michelin Guide "I Spy Oxford" (£2.50): It's a kind of scavenger hunt with information on Oxford's highlights and various activities.

COTSWOLD WILDLIFE PARK (124 A3) (*ω O*)

A combination of zoo and safari park, best explored by car (30 km/18.6 mi from Oxford). Giraffes, rhinos, lions and much more. *Apr–Oct 10am–6pm (and later in the season until it gets dark)* | *£15 adults, £10 children aged 3–6 years* | *Bradwell Grove, Burford* | *www.cotswoldwildlifepark.co.uk*

CUTTESLOWE PARK
(124 B3) (*ω O*)

There aren't many playgrounds in Oxford, but its biggest park (and former vegetable field) has three of them! There's wet fun in the Splash'n'Play, a miniature railway *(Apr–Oct | www.cosme.org.uk/timetable.html)*, mini golf, orienteering, tennis, fitness boot camp *(Tue, Sat 9.30am–10.30am, Wed 9.30am–10.30am and 6pm–7pm)*, skater park, balloon flights *(Apr–Oct, www.adventureballoons.co.uk/oxfordshire-balloon-flights)*, cricket, table tennis, football, beach volleyball and basketball. Wow...! Even listing all the activities leaves you breathless! *Daily* | *Bus no. 2, 7D, 17* | *Harbord Road/A40* | *short.travel/oxf20*

DIDCOT RAILWAY CENTRE
(124 B4) (*ω O*)

A train ride with a steam engine: trainspotting dreams come true here. Even Thomas the tank engine and his friends are fans. Just under half an hour by car from Oxford, or you can take the train to Didcot Parkway. *Sat/Sun 10.30am–4pm, plus special events at other times (see website)* | *approx. £9 adults, £8 children, family ticket £30 (4 people)* | *tel. 01235 817200* | *www.didcotrailwaycentre.org.uk*

Scavenger hunt in a museum, arts and crafts, get stuck in, touch & feel, let off steam: creative activities for little ones

HARRY POTTER TOUR (125 D4) (*M* F7)
If being in Oxford has really got you in the mood for Harry Potter, you can book a tour of the Warner Brothers Studios near London (80 km/49.7 mi from Oxford). Props, backdrops, merchandising. For some sheer horror, for others seventh heaven! Booking in advance is essential. *£39 adults, £31 children and teens aged 5–15 years, family ticket £126, audio guide £4.95 per person | Studio Tour Drive, Leavesden | 1 hr by motorway from Oxford or shuttlebus from Watford train station | tel. 0345 084 0900 | www. wbstudiotour.co.uk*

HINKSEY POOL (122 B6) (*M* F8)
Oxford's iconic "lido" has been something of a people magnet in the summers ever since it first opened in 1934. There is a paddling pool next door (admission free), and a café and picnic area on the site. *Apr–Sep | £6.20 adults, £4.10 children Family ticket (5 people) £18.40 | Lake Street (off Abingdon Road)*

KARTING OXFORD (124 B3) (*M* O)
Children (from 8 years) and adults can race on the winding race course. Book in advance! *Sun–Fri 10am–10pm, Sat 9am–6pm (or until it gets dark), no children's karting on Sat | Children's karting from £15/15min | Oxford Stadium, Sandy Lane | tel. 01865 717134 | www.kartingoxford.co.uk*

STORY MUSEUM (122 B4) (*M* F7)
In a colourful old urban villa, stories have been lovingly prepared for children from the age of two. Join in, touch, dress up and listen. Children's book exchange: bring one you no longer need and take another one home with you! It's worth coming just for the pretty little *café (Tue–Sat 10am–5pm, Sun 11am–4pm)* and shop: where else will you find children's tapas? *Fri/Sat 10am–5pm, Sun 11am–4pm, daily during the school holidays (Oxford) | £7.50 adults, £5 children (from 2 years) Family ticket £20 | 42 Pembroke Street | tel. 01865 790050 | www.story museum.org.uk*

FESTIVALS & EVENTS

Michaelmas, Hilary and Trinity aren't Beckham children, but the university terms: autumn (October–December), spring (January–March) and summer (April–June). Term time or not can often make a difference to opening times. To find out what's happening when, go to the *What's on* pages of the *www.oxford times.co.uk*, Oxford's weekly newspaper.

EVENTS

JANUARY–MARCH

End of Jan: *M@sh Marathon:* Brand new, experimental music by innovative composers, e.g. "Duet for Cello and Waste Bin". *Approx. £5 | Jacqueline du Pré Building, St Hilda's College | www.ox.ac. uk/event/msh-marathon-0*

Mid-Feb: *Turl Arts:* Workshops, performances and art by professors and students at the Turl Street college trio (Jesus, Lincoln & Exeter). *www.turlarts.org*

Early March *Torpids*: College rowing regatta from Donnington Bridge to Folly Bridge

End of March/early April: *Oxford Literary Festival*, top-class bookworm bonanza. Big name writers, creative writing workshops, special offers (for children and adults). *www.oxfordliteraryfestival.org*

APRIL–JUNE

Around Easter: *Oxford and Cambridge Boat Race* on the Thames in London, between Putney and Mortlake. Iconic rowing competition between the university teams of the two arch rivals; since 1829. *www.theboatraces.org*

Mid-April: *Oxford City Bumps Races:* Same rowing course as for the Bumps, but in a fours instead of an eight. *short. travel/oxf25*

1 May: *May Day:* Early-morning singing from Magdalen College Tower

End of May: *Summer Eights:* College rowing regatta from Folly Bridge to Iffley Lock

End of May/early June: *Oxford Pride Parade:* the LGBTQ festival ends with a colourful parade through the city centre. *www.oxford-pride.org.uk*

Oxford Artweek: Week-long "open house" with artists in Oxford and the surrounding area *www.artweeks.org*

End of June: *Encaenia:* Official Latin ceremony awarding honorary doctorates at the Sheldonian Theatre. Pure Oxford: the festive procession with academic robes and mortar boards.

Early June: *Pooh Sticks Championships:* following in the paw prints of Winnie the Pooh, participants lean over a bridge and drop sticks into the water – the winner

How Oxford paints the town red – festive, whimsical, sporting and always plenty of culture

is the person whose stick is first to come out the other side. *Langel Common, Witney | www.pooh-sticks.com*

JULY–SEPTEMBER

Early July: *Alice's Day:* Usually free, offers fun events on everything Alice in Wonderland. *short.travel/oxf26*

Early July: *Cowley Road Carnival:* Oxford's *big day out!* Brilliant street party with a procession, music, dancing, stalls and costumes. *www.cowleyroadcarnival.co.uk*

End of July: *Truck Festival:* Where would you meet musicians like the Libertines, Idris Elba and the Oxford Symphony Orchestra? At the iconic music event in Hill Farm. *www.truckfestival.com*

End of July/early Aug: *Folly Fest:* Live Music Festival. Free! *www.follyfest.co.uk*

Mid-Aug: *Oxford City Royal Regatta:* Folk festival-like rowing regatta with the finishing straight in Longbridges. *short.travel/27*

1st Mon/Tue after the first Sun in Sept: *St Giles Fair:* Traditional street fair

Early Sept: *Oxford Open Doors:* Free admission to many special buildings. *short.travel/oxf28*

OCTOBER–DECEMBER

End of Oct. *Campaign for Real Ale Oxford Beer & Cider Festival:* Highly enjoyable festival celebrating real ale and cider! In-house magazine with the best name: The Oxford Drinker. *www.oxford.camra.org.uk*

End of Nov: *Oxford Festival of Lights:* Light festival with art and cultural events

Christmas Market: On Broad Street and around the castle

PUBLIC HOLIDAYS

1 Jan	New Year's Day
March/April	Good Friday, Easter Monday
1st Mon in May	Bank holiday
Last Mon in May	Bank holiday
Last Mon in Aug	Bank holiday
25/26 Dec	Christmas

LINKS, BLOGS, APPS & MORE

www.dailyinfo.co.uk More than an information point: the Oxford guide Daily Info is a treasure trove of amusing reviews of restaurants and cultural events, top tips for locals, visitors and students, and an Oxford picture gallery that is well worth seeing. Attractive, practical and good!

www.independentoxford.com No chains allowed – all the indie shops at a glance, compiled by the bloggers Anna (@AnnaLMunday) and Rosie (@ARosieLifeStore). Twice a year: **INSIDER TIP** Instameet! Photogenic Instagram walk through Oxford with creative minds from the social media scene

www.bittenoxford.co.uk Slow food is in – if you like cultivated eating and drinking, please take a look at Bitten! Jacqui (@foodieontour) and Becca (@Ox_Bex) collect brutally honest reviews and information by foodies for foodies

www.indieoxfordcompendium.com Brand new co-production between Bitten and IndieOxford. The little grey book (£4) is your bible for individual shops, bars and restaurants with that extra special touch

blog.oxforddictionaries.com The home of the English language dictionary is in Oxford – and everyday it blogs about new things, entertaining things, and developments in the English language to make you think

www.oxfordshirebloggers. co.uk Bundled under the heading of Entertainment, Food, Days out and Shops, you'll find individual blog posts with unusual tips and personal recommendations from Oxford locals

@smartOxford "Jonny Oxford" tweets bizarre, popular and invariably interesting morsels from and about Oxford

Regardless of whether you are still researching your trip or are already in Oxford: these addresses will provide you with more information, videos and networks to make your holiday even more enjoyable

VIDEOS & MUSIC

@OxTweets Interesting facts, current topics, points of interest – the Oxford info account with the most followers

www.youtube.com/user/OxfordUnion Debates are held at the Oxford Union in Frewin Court, with speakers ranging from David Hasselhoff to Julian Assange. Very difficult for outsiders to get in – but that's not a problem, as it now has a YouTube channel!

www.youtube.com/user/oxford Official but very entertaining YouTube channel on everything to do with the university – lectures, research, places, professors and students

www.oxfordmusic.xyz The ABC of the Oxford indie music scene. Warning: leaves you longing for live gigs!

APPS

Oxford University: The Official Guide app Official Oxford University app with news, stories, events, walking tours and Near Me feature: sights in your area (only for iOS)

Mobile Oxford Lots of practical information on the university and city

Explore Oxford University Museums app The Oxford museums app: current topics, events, visitor info, top highlights

Oxford Bus app from the Oxford Bus Company. Tickets for City, Park&Ride, X90, Airline and Thames Travel

The Dealer app Brilliant app created by the former students Ed and Henry: Oxford bars, clubs and restaurants announce their special offers on the app – free for users, and parts of the proceeds are donated to the homeless charity. Go out, save money – and contribute to a good cause! Brilliant idea!

TRAVEL TIPS

ARRIVAL

✈ Only student pilots and multi-millionaires land at Oxford Airport. Mere mortals fly to Heathrow, Gatwick, Stansted or Luton. The airports are served by buses: from Heathrow and Gatwick it's the Airline Coach: from Heathrow every 30min, travel time 1½hrs; from Gatwick: hourly, travel time 2½hrs. (www.airline.oxfordbus.co.uk). National Express buses travel between Oxford and Stansted, and Oxford and Luton (www.nationalexpress.com).

🚆 From the continent by Eurostar to London *(www.eurostar.com)*, then on from Paddington (every half-hour, travel time 1hr). Trains to Oxford Parkway to the north run from Marylebone via Bicester Village.

🚗 From Dover (at least 3hrs away), take the M20 towards London, then the M25 clockwise to the M40. Oxford is about 13 km/8.1 mi west of M40 (coming from the south: exit at Junction 8).

🚌 The Oxford Tube *(www.oxfordtube. com)* is not an underground train, but a coach that runs to London every 15mins. Fares cost £15 from London to Oxford (approx. 1½ hrs.). WiFi and USB connections. The X90 offer from the Oxford Bus Company is similar (x90.oxfordbus.co.uk).

BANKS

Banks are usually open 9.30am–4.30pm on workdays and generally closed on holidays. Most banks have cash machines (ATMs) available for their customers.

BICYCLES

Hire, accessories, repairs, route suggestions, guided tours and cycling holidays – the popular bicycle shop *Bainton Bikes* in Jericho takes care of it all! *Mon–Fri 8.45am–5.30pm, Sat 9am–5pm, Sun 10am–4pm | Bicycle hire £10/day, £18/3 days | tel. 01865 311610 | Walton Street Cycles, 78 Walton Street | www.bainton bikes.com* You can also get a Bainton's bicycle by smartphone using the *Donkey app (www. donkey.bike)*: register online, pay with your credit card, then use the code to release the bike from one of the *docking stations (£8.40/6hrs., £12/24hrs.).* *Oxonbikes* is a city-wide fleet of pedal and electric bikes. You can obtain them from and return them to 16 (unmanned) stations. Register online free (with a credit card). *£1/hr., e-bikes £2/hr. | tel. 01865 238013 | www.oxonbikes.co.uk*

RESPONSIBLE TRAVEL

It doesn't take a lot to be environmentally friendly whilst travelling. Don't just think about your carbon footprint whilst flying to and from your holiday destination, but also about how you can protect nature and culture abroad. As a tourist it is especially important to respect nature, look out for local products, cycle instead of driving, save water and much more. If you would like to find out more about eco-tourism please visit: *www.ecotourism.org*

From arrival to weather

Your holiday from start to finish: the most important addresses and information for your trip to Oxford

CONSULATES AND EMBASSIES

EMBASSY OF IRELAND
17 Grosvenor Place| Belgravia | London | www.dfa.ie/irish-embassy/great-britain | tel. 020 7235 2171

HIGH COMMISSION OF AUSTRALIA
Strand | London | www.uk.embassy.gov.au | tel. 020 7379 4334

HIGH COMMISSION OF CANADA
Canada House | Trafalgar Square | London | www.canadainternational.gc.ca/united_kingdom-royaume_uni/index.aspx?lang=eng | tel. 020 7004 6000

U.S. EMBASSY
24 Grosvenor Square | London | uk.usembassy.gov | tel. 020 7499 9000

CUSTOMS

Arriving from EU countries you can import items for your personal use without paying any duty (e.g. 800 cigarettes, 10 l of spirits). There are different allowances for arrivals from outside the EU, for information check: *www.gov.uk/browse/abroad/travel-abroad*

DRIVING

In the UK you drive on the left. At *roundabouts,* traffic coming from the right has priority. The problem you will have with a car in Oxford is: where to park? Best option: go to a Park-and-Ride car park. There are several of them all around Oxford *(all open 24/7)*: Pear Tree, Oxford Parkway (north); Redbridge (south); Thornhill (east); Seacourt (west). Pay at the machine (£2 per day) or by credit card (online/phone £2.20). The bus ticket to the city is separate, and there are several options. A *return ticket* that will get you into the city and back again, for instance, costs £2.80 at peak times. If you park at Redbridge car park and want to do a "Hop-on-hop-off" bus tour, get on the green double-decker for the *Meadows & Bridges* tour (see Round trips).
If a hotel has parking facilities, it's something special and will usually be mentioned on the website. Still, be sure to find out for certain – often parking has to be booked as an extra.

ELECTRICITY

Mains voltage: 240 volt/50 Hz. Sockets have three holes, and the matching plugs have *three pins*. You will need an

BUDGETING

Beer	£3.90/$4.90
	for 1 pint at a pub
Fish & chips	£7.70/$9.70
	to take away
Souvenir	£8.80/$11.20
	mug with a college symbol
Cinema	£8.80/$11.20
	per person (not 3D)
Public transport	£4.40/$5.60
	for a day ticket on the bus
Taxi	£8.80/$11.20
	per mile

adapter. Don't forget to switch on the socket when you charge your phone: they all have a switch.

EMERGENCY SERVICES

Emergency control centre *999*. You must give your name first, and then you will be asked, *"Which service do you require?"*. You then ask either for an *ambulance*, the *fire service* or the *police*.

HEALTH

In an emergency, dial *999* for an *ambulance*. European nationals with a EHIC card can receive treatment through the National Health Service (NHS) at *doctors' surgeries* and hospitals. At the time of going to press, the EHIC (European Health Insurance) card was still being accepted. Information number in the event of illness (not in an emergency unless affecting the teeth): *111*. Emergency department: *Accident & Emergency (A&E) | John Radcliffe Hospital | Headley Way | Headington | tel. 03003 047777 | www. ouh.nhs.uk/hospitals/jr*

The *Midnight Pharmacy (150 Oxford Road | tel. 01865 770121)* is open until midnight Wed to Sat, and until 9pm Sun.

IMMIGRATION

For citizens of most EU countries, including Ireland, an ID card is sufficient. US citizens as well as citizens from the commonwealth need a valid passport; there is no requirement for a visa for stays up to 6 months. If you are coming by car,

FOR BOOKWORMS AND FILM BUFFS

The Bone Season – the first book (2013) in the fantasy series by the Oxford student Samantha Shannon *(www. samantha-shannon.blogspot.co.uk)*. A map and other information make it as clear as daylight: the fictional penal colony Sheol I is a thinly disguised Oxford. Clairvoyant Paige is banned because of her supernatural senses. What follows is a forbidden love story with her "Warden", Arcturus. Blood sovereign Nashira becomes suspicious... soon to be released as a film

Alice in Wonderland – a must read! THE iconic book (1865) to beat all others. Lewis Carroll immortalised several Oxford curiosities in his most famous work. Surreal, brilliant, often imitated: but nothing is as good as the original

Morse/Lewis/Endeavour – scene of the crime: Oxford. Iconic crime series since 1987, based on the novels of Colin Dexter. In the 1990s it was Inspector Morse who kept Oxford in check, while his sidekick Lewis was later given nine seasons of his own. Endeavour brings us the young Morse in 1960s Oxford. Essential viewing for any Oxford fan

The Riot Club – film version of Laura Wade's play "Posh". Satire on the (in)famous Bullingdon Club of privileged Oxford *toffs*. A wild party goes out of control – with plenty of violence. The perpetrators are arrested – but can we be sure they will be held to account?

you will need your driver's license, your vehicle registration documents and the "Green Card", the international insurance card.

INFORMATION

OXFORD VISITOR INFORMATION CENTRE (122 B3) (*M F6*)

Information on guided tours, accommodation and excursions. There is a range of free brochures at the back of the shop. *Sep–June Mon–Sat 9.30am–5pm, Sun 10am–4pm, Jul/Aug. Mon–Sat 9am–5.30pm, Sun 9.30am–4pm | 15–16 Broad Street | tel. 01865 686430 | www.experienceoxfordshire.org*

INTERNET & WIFI

Internet (Wi-Fi) access is free in most hotels, cafés, restaurants etc. The password is usually somewhere in clear sight, otherwise just ask for the code. You'll be in luck if you're a member of the Eduroam network: because so many university institutions are scattered over the city, your device will often log you in automatically and free of charge.

LOST & FOUND

Oxford Bus Company lost and found helpline: tel. 01865 785400. For insurance reasons, report all losses to the police.

PHONE & MOBILE PHONE

Phone boxes accept credit cards and coins. The dial code for Great Britain is 0044. When calling from abroad, omit the '0' of the area code (01865 for Oxford) or the first zero on mobile numbers. The UK dialling code for the USA and Canada is 001, for Australia 0061, and for Ireland 00353. Omit any leading '1'

CURRENCY CONVERTER

US$	GBP	GBP	US$
1	0.75	10	13.30
2	1.50	20	26.60
3	2.25	25	33.25
4	3.00	30	39.90
5	3.75	40	53.20
6	4.50	50	66.50
7	5.25	70	93.10
8	6.00	80	106.40
9	6.75	95	126.35

For current exchange rates see www.xe.com

in North American numbers and any first zero in Australian or Irish numbers. Operator: within the UK 100, international 155. SIM cards, prepaid cards and vouchers for mobile phones are available from *phone shops* (e.g. Carphone Warehouse, Vodafone, O2, Three, T-Mobile), and from supermarkets and *corner shops*.

POST

Sending postcards and letters within Europe: £1.05. Stamps are available when you buy your postcards from souvenir shops. Small *post offices* are often tucked away in other shops. *Main post office (122 B3) (M F6) | 102–104 St Aldates | Mon, Wed–Sat 9am–5.30, Tue 9.30am–5pm*

PRICES & CURRENCY

Compared with continental Europe, shopping and going out is expensive in the UK. A lot of the museums are free, but if there is a charge, then it's often steep. The tax on fuel and luxury goods is especially high.

The currency is the pound sterling (£), and one pound is made up of 100 pence (called "p" for short). Withdrawing cash from an ATM or *cash point* on a foreign bank card will incur a charge. The most common credit cards are Visa and Mastercard.

PUBLIC TRANSPORT

The *Oxford Bus Company* drives the city routes, services the Park-and-Ride car parks, London and Heathrow and Gatwick airports. *Travel shops:* (122 A3) *(m E6)* | 89 Gloucester Green (Mon–Fri 7am–7pm, Sat 8am–6pm, Sun 8am–4pm); (122 C3) *(m G6)* | 44–45 High Street (Mon–Fri 8am–4pm, Sat 8am–4pm | tel. 01865 785400 | www.oxfordbus.co.uk. App, timetable and tickets are available online. If you are planning to stay longer, it might be worth obtaining a top-up *Key Smartcard* (www.oxfordkey.co.uk/smart-card). A *Smartzone Day Pass* (£4.20) is also valid on *Stagecoach* (www.stagecoachbus.com) buses and *Thames Travel* (www.thames-travel.co.uk) in the city. What time is the bus? Real-time information on public transport: *www.oxontime.com*

Megabus (www.uk.megabus.com) and *National Express* (www.nationalexpress.com) will take you to other cities.

SIGHTSEEING & GUIDED TOURS

There are plenty of guided tours, and you can also book "Official Walking Tours" through the *Visitor Centre*. A lot of other providers on Broad Street will approach you, wanting to sell you "the best Oxford tour". You might be lucky, you might not! Go by the individual's personality: Is your potential tour guide friendly? Funny? Does he or she amuse you with wacky anecdotes? Then it might not be something to base a doctoral thesis on, but you can be sure of having a highly entertaining tour.

WEATHER IN OXFORD

	Jan	Feb	March	April	May	June	July	Aug	Sept	Oct	Nov	Dec
Daytime temperature in °C/°F	6/43	7/45	10/50	13/55	17/63	20/68	22/72	21/70	19/66	14/57	10/50	7/45
Night-time temperatures in °C/°F	2/36	2/36	3/37	5/41	8/46	11/52	13/55	13/55	11/52	8/46	5/41	3/37
Sunshine hours/day	2	2	4	6	7	7	7	6	5	3	2	1
Precipitation days/month	11	9	8	8	8	8	9	9	9	9	10	9

One ghostly but fun experience is **INSIDERTIP** *Bill Spectre's Ghost Trail:* With plenty of spooky dramatics, Bill will take you around Oxford's creepiest spots *(Fri/Sat 6.30 from the castle, 6.50pm from 15/16 Broad Street | £9 | tel. 07941 041811 | www.ghosttrail.org).* The open-topped ● double-decker bus runs on two routes (red: *City & University,* green: *Meadows & Bridges*), covering all the sights *(Apr–Oct 9.30am–5pm every 10–15mins, less often in winter | Day ticket (valid on both lines) £15, can be combined with other attractions; tickets on the bus, also e.g. from hotels or the Visitor Centre | Audio commentary in 11 languages, new: commentary for children | www.citysightseeingoxford.com).* You can get on and off as often as you like with the ticket.

No Oxford experience is complete without a ● boat trip! They always start from Folly Bridge. *Salter's Steamers* chug to Iffley lock and back in 40 mins *(Apr–Oct | £8),* and also have jazz cruises with a Captain's Barbecue on the programme *(£48 | tel. 01865 243421 | www.salters steamers.co.uk). Oxford River Cruises* offer various lovely trips, such as the *Pimm's Cruise (Apr–Oct | 1hr, £29 per person)* or the *Mad Hatter's Tea Party (2hrs | £39 per person)* with sandwiches and... tea! *(both trips from 8 people, others from 1 person | tel. 0845 226 9396 | www.oxforddrivercruises.com).*

On the *Official Oxford Cycling Tour (£21 | duration 2–3hrs)* you'll see the main sights from your bike, travelling at a comfortable speed. Entertaining and informative commentary, and comfortable bikes. Book through the Visitor Centre (see p. 112) or through Bainton Bikes (see p. 108).

TAXI

You'll find the typical black taxis *(Hackney cabs)* in Oxford as well as London. If the yellow light on the roof is on, then you can pretend you're in a film, stick out your arm and step out into the road, calling, "Taxi!" – which is called *hailing a cab.* There are taxi ranks at the station, on Gloucester Green, St Giles and at Carfax. A black cab will hold 5 to 6 people, fewer with suitcases. The city council decides the fares *(short.travel/oxf29).* The current charge for vomiting in the vehicle: £30. Pre-ordered taxis (ordinary cars) are a little cheaper, e.g. *ABC Radio Taxis (tel. 01865 242424 | www.abcradiotaxis.co.uk)* or *Oxford Cars (tel. 01865 406070 | www.oxfordcars.co.uk).* Mike John and Mark Hatters' *Go Green Taxis* ⊗ *(tel. 01865 922222 | www.gogreentaxisltd.co.uk)* is an environmentally-friendly company. The taxi apps are on the websites.

TIME

Greenwich Mean Time (GMT) is one hour behind Central European Time all year round. End of March to the end of October: daylight saving time, with the clocks changing on the same dates as most European countries.

TIPPING

Always look closely at the bill: the *service charge/tip* is sometimes simply added to it, but not always. Sometimes the menu says: *service not included.* In a pub, you order at the bar and don't tip. If you're sitting at a table, you can leave some change on the table after you've paid. The usual amount is 10–15 percent for good service.

STREET ATLAS

The green line indicates the Discovery Tour "Oxford at a glance"
The blue line indicates all other Discovery Tours

All tours are also marked on the pull-out map

Photo: Oxford as seen from South Park

Exploring Oxford

The map on the back cover shows how the area has been sub-divided

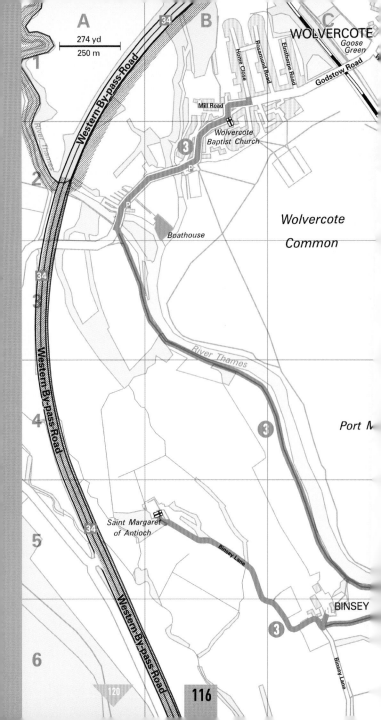

WOLVERCOTE

Goose
Green

34

274 yd
250 m

Western By-pass Road

River Thames

1

Home Close

Rosamund Road

Elmthorpe Road

Godstow Road

Mill Road

3

Wolvercote
Baptist Church

P

2

34

P

Boathouse

Wolvercote

Common

3

River Thames

4

3

Port M

Western By-pass Road

Saint Margaret
of Antioch

34

Binsey Lane

5

BINSEY

3

Binsey Lane

6

Carlton Road
Wolsey Road
Scho
D
E
Blandford Ave.
Davenant Road
Cavendish Road
Southdale Road
Jackson Road
Buckler Road
Scott Road
First Turn
4144
Summertown
House Mansion
Upland Park Road
Wentworth Road
Aldrich Road
Islip Road
Woodstock Road
Salisbury Cr.
Primary
School
Apsley Road
Hernes Road
Harpes Ro
Saint Peters Road
St Gregory's and
St Augustine's Church
Field Ho.
Paddox Lane
Field Ho. Dr.
Canal Close
Victoria Road
Kings Cross Road
Middle Way
Squitchey Lane
Summerhill Road
Hamilton Road
Uffgar Road
Blenheim Drive
Richards Lane
Hobson Road
Portland Road
Lonsdale Ro
Saint Edward's
School Golf
Course
Bishop Kirk
Place
Osberton Road
Grove Street
Rogers Street
Rogers Street
4165
k Meadow
Library
Summ
Fields
ford
y Boundary
ne
Oxford Canal
South Parade
Summerfield
Road
St. Edward's
School
St Edward's Avenue
Strafield Road
Banbury Road
3
Oakthorpe Road
Ferry Pool Rd
Keble College
Sports
Ground
Thorncliffe Road
Beechcroft Road
4144
Burgess
Field
Lark Hill
Moreton Road
Elizabeth Jennings Way
Lathbury Road
Staverton Road
Cunliffe
Stone Meadow
St. John's
College
Sports
Ground
Woodstock
4
Bainton Road
Be
Finchley Road
University
College
Annexe
Chalfont Road
Hayfield Road
Rawlinson Road
Philip
and James
School
Burgess Mead
Polstead Road
5
Trap Ground
Allotments
Aristotle Lane
St Margaret's Road
Saint Margaret's
Church
Plater Drive
Saint
Margaret's Road
St Hugh's
College
Farndon Road
WALTON MANOR
Steven's
Cl.
Canter-
bury
Rd.
St
Winchester
Wlk.
Willow
The Cres.
Southmoor
Pl.
Kingston
Tackley
Pl.
Warn-
borough
Butler
Sch.
Rd.
St. Anthonys
College
Walk
Rusher
Southmoor Rd.
Lodge
Rd.
Lonsworth
Rd.
Leckford
Road
Road
Winchester
Rd.
St.
Bernards
3
117
121
Walton Well Rd.
St.
Banbury Road

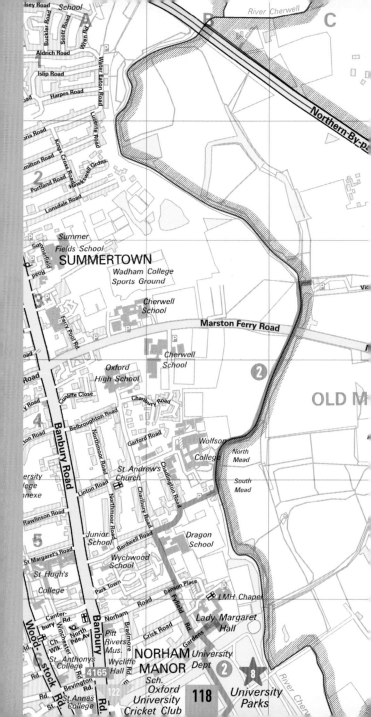

D **E** **F** Pennywell Wood

1

ELSFIELD

274 yd
250 m

2

420

3

Park Way

Lodge Close

Mill Lane

Ponds Lane

Butts Lane

nt Nicholas Church MARSTON

Elsfield Road

Elsfield Road

420 Northern By-pass Road

ry Road

Court Place
Farm Allotments

Court
Place
Farm

ON

Oxford Road

olas
ool

Library

Oxford Road

Boults Lane

4

Horseman Close

Elms Drive

Marsh Lane

New Marston
Primary
School

Shockleys Rd

Northway
Centre

Borrowmead Road

Millfield Road

Westlands Drive

Sutton Road

Goose Lane

Stanefield
Road

John R

Haynes Road

Raymund Road

Oxford Road

Cherwell Drive

Gordon Close

Rylands

Ewin Close

Copse Lane

5

endish Drive

Road

The Link

Mortimer Drive

Lewell
Avenue

Nicholas
Avenue

Beechey Avenue

Old Marston Road

Ouseley Close

Derwent Avenue

Coniston Avenue

Bowness Avenue

Headley Way

Ambleside Drive

Eden Drive

Rippington Drive

W MARSTON

Farmer
Place

Crescent

Crotch
Hadow
Rd

Jack Straws Lane

St.Joseph
Catholic
Primary
School

Saint Anthony
of Padua

John Radcliffe
Children's
Hospital

6

rtford
Ground

ark
arm

Goodson Wk

Purcell Road

Parry
Cl.

West
Cl.

Hugh

Nicholson
Rd.

Croft
Cl.

Staines
Pl.

Heather
Pl.

Vernon
Pl.

Weldon

Hayes Cl.

Marston
Road

Jack

Straws

Lynn Cl.

D
Field
Cl.

Lane

Milham Ford
Upper
School

Mead

Headley Way

Staunton Road

Playing
Field

119

123

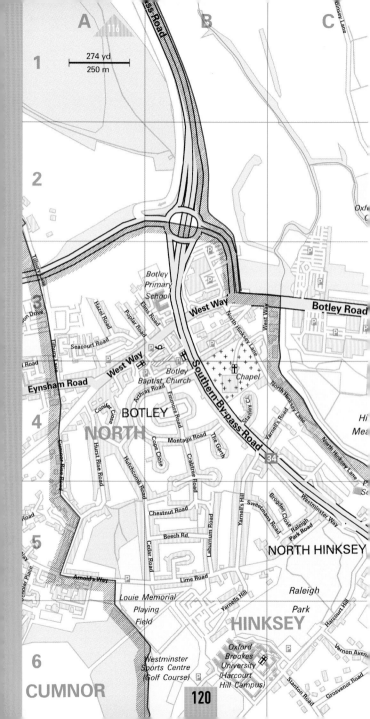

1

274 yd
250 m

2

ss Road

Oxf

Botley Road

3

Botley
Primary
School

West Way

Seacourt Road

West Way

North Hinksey Lane

West Way

Hazel Road

Poplar Road

Elms Road

Eynsham Road

Botley
Baptist Church

Arthray Road

Chapel

North Hinksey Lane

4

BOTLEY

NORTH

Conifer Close

Finmore Road

Montagu Road

The Garth

Crabtree Road

Cope Close

Hurst Rise Road

Hutchcomb Road

Raleigh Cl

Yarnell's Road

North Hinksey Lane

Southern By-pass Road

34

Hi
Mea

Yarnell's Hill

Sweetmans Road

Brookon Close

Westminster Way

Raleigh
Park Road

So

Chestnut Road

Beech Rd.

Laburnum Road

Cedar Road

Lime Road

5

Arnold's Way

Louie Memorial
Playing
Field

Yarnells Hill

NORTH HINKSEY

Raleigh

Park

HINKSEY

Scholar Place

Westminster
Sports Centre
(Golf Course)

Oxford
Brookes
University
(Harcourt
Hill Campus)

Harcourt Hill

Vernon Aven

Stanton Road

Grosvenor Road

6

CUMNOR

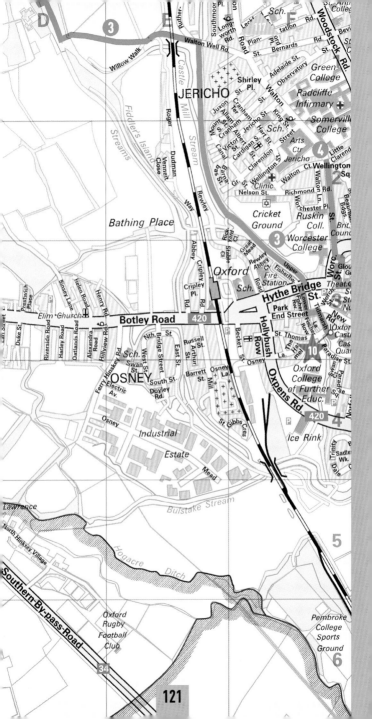

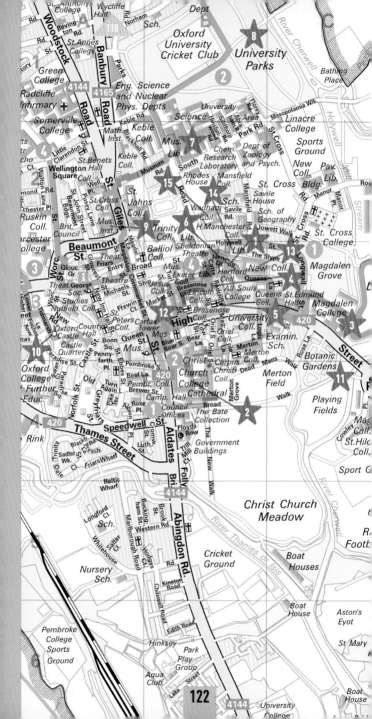

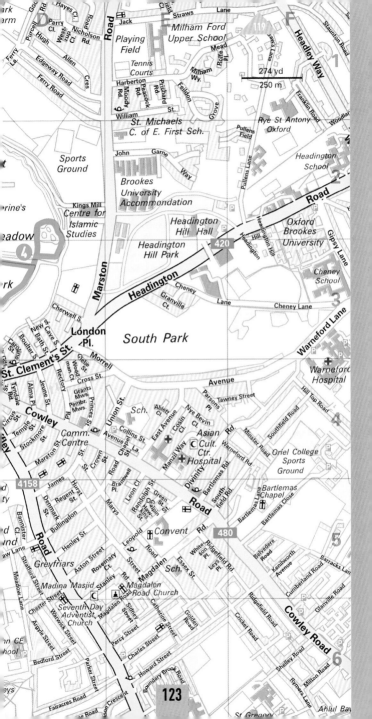

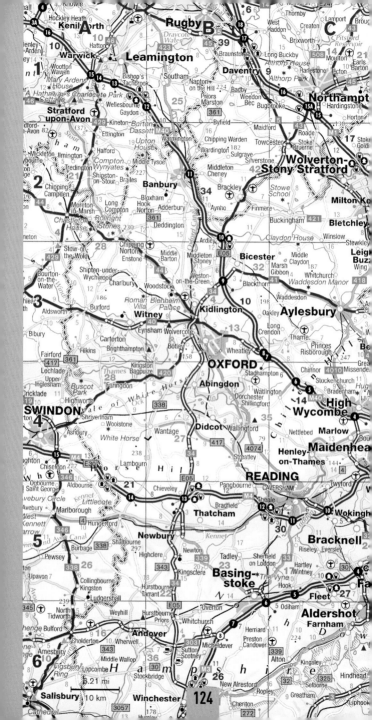

This index lists a selection of streets and squares shown on the street atlas

Motorway / Autobahn		Autoroute / Autosnelweg
Road with four lanes / Vierspurige Straße		Route à quatre voies / Weg met vier rijstroken
Through road / Durchgangsstraße		Route de transit / Weg voor doorgaand verkeer
Main road / Hauptstraße		Route principale / Hoofdweg
Other roads / Sonstige Straßen		Autres routes / Overige wegen
Information - Parking / Information - Parkplatz		Information - Parking / Informatie - Parkeerplaats
One way road / Einbahnstraße		Rue à sens unique / Straat met eenrichtingsverkeer
Pedestrian zone / Fußgängerzone		Zone piétonne / Voetgangersgebied
Main railway with station / Hauptbahn mit Bahnhof		Chemin de fer principal avec gare / Belangrijke spoorweg met station
Other railways / Sonstige Bahnen		Autres lignes / Overige spoorwegen
Hospital - Hotel - Youth hostel / Krankenhaus - Hotel - Jugendherberge		Hôpital - Hôtel - Auberge de jeunesse / Ziekenhuis - Hotel - Jeugdherberg
Monument - Tower / Denkmal - Turm		Monument - Tour / Monument - Toren
Landing place / Anlegestelle		Embarcadère / Aanlegplaats
Church - Church of interest - Synagogue / Kirche - Sehenswerte Kirche - Synagoge		Église - Église remarquable - Synagogue / Kerk - Bezienswaardige kerk - Synagoge
Post office - Police station / Postamt - Polizei		Bureau de poste - Police / Postkantoor - Politie

Built-up area - Public buildings / Bebauung - Öffentliche Gebäude		Zone bâtie - Bâtiments public / Woongebied - Openbaar gebouw
Industrial area / Industriegebiet		Zone industrielle / Industriekomplex
Park, forest - Cemetery / Park, Wald - Friedhof		Parc, bois - Cimetière / Park, bos - Begraafplaats
Restricted traffic zone / Zone mit Verkehrsbeschränkungen		Circulation réglementée par des péages / Zone met verkeersbeperkingen
MARCO POLO Discovery Tour 1 / MARCO POLO Erlebnistour 1		MARCO POLO Tour d'aventure 1 / MARCO POLO Avontuurlijke Route 1
MARCO POLO Discovery Tours / MARCO POLO Erlebnistouren		MARCO POLO Tours d'aventure / MARCO POLO Avontuurlijke Routes
MARCO POLO Highlight		MARCO POLO Highlight

FOR YOUR NEXT TRIP...

MARCO POLO TRAVEL GUIDES

INDEX

All sights and destinations mentioned in this guide are listed in this index. Page numbers in bold refer to the main entry.